SCHOLASTIC

YEAR IN SPORTS 2013

Scholastic Inc.

Copyright © 2012 by Shoreline Publishing Group LLC

All rights reserved. Published by Scholastic Inc., *Publishers since 1920*.
SCHOLASTIC and associated logos are trademarks and/or registered trademarks of Scholastic Inc.

No part of this publication may be reproduced, stored in a retrieval system, or transmitted in any form or by any means, electronic, mechanical, photocopying, recording, or otherwise, without written permission of the publisher. For information regarding permission, write to Scholastic Inc., Attention: Permissions Department, 557 Broadway, New York, NY, 10012.

ISBN 978-0-545-42520-9

10 9 8 7 6 5 4 3 2 1   12 13 14 15 16

Printed in the U.S.A.   40
First edition, December 2012

Produced by Shoreline Publishing Group LLC

Due to the publication date, records, results, and statistics are current as of August 2012.

UNAUTHORIZED: This book is not sponsored by or affiliated with the athletes, teams, or anyone involved with them.

CONTENTS

Let the Games Begin!

The Opening Ceremonies of the London Olympics featured the five rings in a shower of sparks.

The past year in sports was dominated by the Olympics, so we'll take a page from their book to open ours. Please take a seat and enjoy the ***Scholastic Year in Sports*** Opening Ceremonies!

Since the United States is our host country, our ceremonies begin with a music-and-dance number honoring our favorite sports. The show starts with a crew of dancers all wearing helmets and shoulder pads making their way into the stadium, while a marching band plays "Take Me Out to the Ball Game." The band is followed by 300 kids, all bouncing basketballs with pictures of **LeBron James** painted on them. Next, led by the gold-medal-winning U.S. women's soccer team, 150 kids are dribbling soccer balls. **Michael Phelps** is swimming in a giant portable pool that's being pulled around the stadium by a pack of youth ice-hockey players. After Phelps, a team of skateboarders is being towed by a NASCAR racing machine as "We Are the Champions" plays on the stadium organ. The fans, of course, are doing the wave.

Following the musical numbers comes everyone's favorite part: the parade of athletes. As you read along in this edition of our annual salute to sports, watch for these heroes and heroines to make their appearances: **Eli Manning**, **Cam Newton**, **David Freese**, **Dwyane Wade**, **Jonathan Quick**, **Jimmie Johnson**, **Dale Earnhardt Jr.**, **Brittney Griner**, **Yani Tseng**, **Tiger Woods**, **Shaun White**, **Roger Federer**, **Serena Williams**, and **Lionel Messi**.

And don't miss Olympic stars such as Phelps, **Gabby Douglas**, **Missy Franklin**, and **Allyson Felix**. Then the teams come marching in, led by the New York Giants, St. Louis Cardinals, Miami Heat, Los Angeles Kings, LSU, Baylor, Kentucky, plus Spain's soccer team.

Our Opening Ceremonies end with the lighting of the torch. Instead of a torch, however, we simply asked hot-hitting **Josh Hamilton** to hold up his bat. (How awesome was this sports year? Hamilton tied a record with four homers in a game . . . and he didn't make our Top 10!).

With the athletes assembled, the torch lit, and the fans ready for action . . . let the games (and the reading) begin!

Hamilton's hot hitting was one for the record books.

MOMENTS IN SPORTS
SEPTEMBER 2011 ▶ AUGUST 2012

The Year in Sports was dominated by the Summer Olympics, so it'll be no surprise that an Olympic feat is No. 1 on our Top 10. In fact, we could have filled the entire Top 10 with Olympic moments, but there were lots of other amazing athletic feats in the past year. But don't worry, we've got a big Summer Olympics section right after this one, so you'll have plenty of ways to re-live those two weeks you spent glued to the screen, cheering on your favorites.

Beyond the Olympics, however, the major pro sports all had thrilling championships of their own. You saw a team win its first-ever title, and a King win his first-ever crown. There was perfection in a college sport, and also in baseball in a very different way.

And along with Olympic heroes, a surprise hero emerged in pro hoops: Did you go Linsane?

It was a busy, memorable, Olympic, awesome, surprising, amazing, and exhausting year. So sit back and relax with a good book . . . and see if your personal Top 10 matched ours.

Let the Games . . . and the reading . . . begin!

10 ***SPAIN GOES FOR THREE*** *Goalie and captain Iker Casillas led his teammates in a victory yell after Spain won the 2012 European Championships of soccer. With a 4–0 win over Italy, Spain can now be called by experts one of the greatest national soccer teams of all time. Spain also won the 2010 World Cup and the previous European title in 2008. Viva España indeed!*

9 PERFECT TIMES THREE With six perfect games in baseball since 2009, it might seem like they happen a lot. Trust us: They don't! In 2012, *Philip Humber* of the White Sox, *Matt Cain* of the Giants, and *Felix Hernandez* of the Mariners (pictured) all threw perfect games. That still makes only 23 in more than 125 years of pro baseball. So even though these came in a trio, they are still really rare!

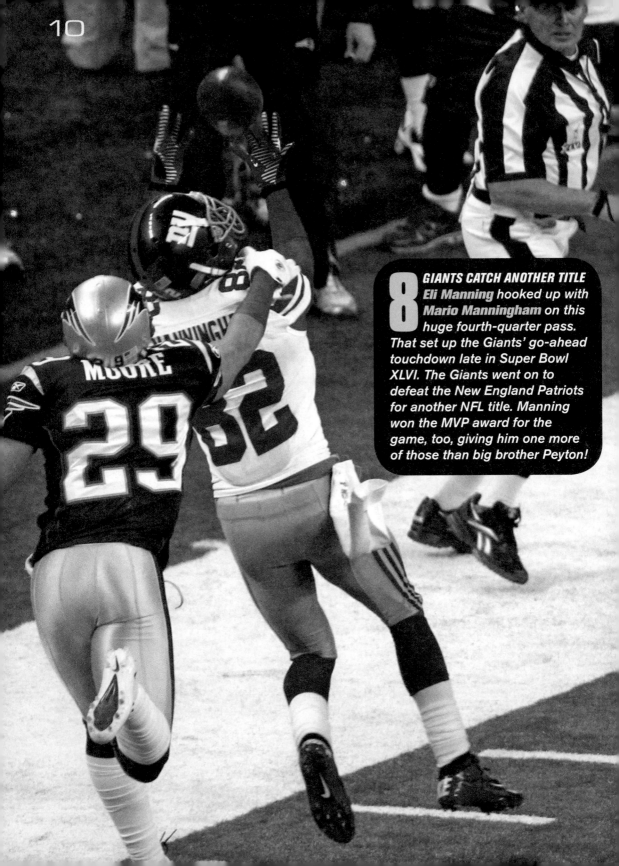

8 **GIANTS CATCH ANOTHER TITLE**
Eli Manning hooked up with *Mario Manningham* on this huge fourth-quarter pass. That set up the Giants' go-ahead touchdown late in Super Bowl XLVI. The Giants went on to defeat the New England Patriots for another NFL title. Manning won the MVP award for the game, too, giving him one more of those than big brother Peyton!

7 LINSANITY In January 2012, just about the only people who had heard of **Jeremy Lin** were his parents and Harvard basketball fans. By the end of February, he was the most famous athlete in America. Lin, then a guard for the Knicks, came out of nowhere to set scoring records and lead the Knicks on a long winning streak. His rise created "Linsanity" wherever he went. (In July, he signed with the Houston Rockets.)

6 **THE HEAT IS ON!**
LeBron James changed teams and joined Miami with one goal: Win an NBA title. In his second season, he achieved it. Dwyane Wade (left), however, had been with Miami for nine years, and it was his second title with the Heat.

5 **BAYLOR: UNDEFEATED!** The Baylor Bears women's basketball team put together one of the most dominant seasons in college sports. The Bears went 41–0 on the way to capturing the school's first national championship in hoops. Star *Brittney Griner* was named the tournament's most outstanding player.

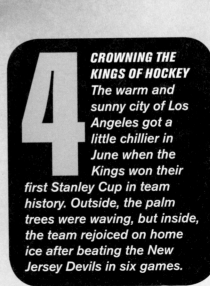

4

CROWNING THE KINGS OF HOCKEY
The warm and sunny city of Los Angeles got a little chillier in June when the Kings won their first Stanley Cup in team history. Outside, the palm trees were waving, but inside, the team rejoiced on home ice after beating the New Jersey Devils in six games.

3

SUPER SOCCER WOMEN! *And now to the Olympics: The most dramatic event for many fans was the exciting semifinal showdown between the U.S. and Canadian women's soccer teams. Canada nearly pulled off an amazing upset, leading three times in the game. The American team never quit, however, coming back time and again. Alex Morgan's header in the 123rd minute gave the U.S. a spot in the gold-medal game, which they won over Japan, 2–1.*

2

PHELPS IS PHANTASTIC The Olympic Games have been held every four years since 1896; the Winter Games were added starting in 1928. Tens of thousands of athletes have done their best to win, but no one has won more than American swimmer *Michael Phelps*. With four golds and two silvers in London, Phelps reached an amazing career total of 18 golds and 22 total medals, both unreachable records.

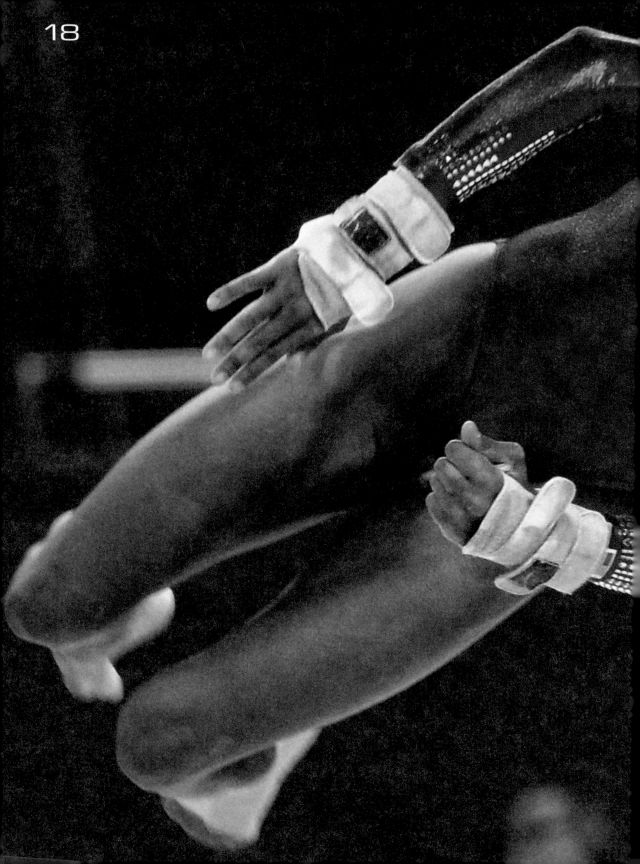

1

GOLDEN GABBY *Talk about pressure: Gabby Douglas came into the women's all-around expected to bring home the gold. With the eyes of the world on her, the 16-year-old with the golden smile did just that. She held the lead through every part of the event and became only the fourth American to win the all-around. She also helped her fellow U.S. gymnasts win the team event for the first time since 1996. Golden Gabby became one of the faces of the Games for American fans.*

OPENING WITH A BANG!
The 2012 Summer Olympic Games opened in London on July 27 with an amazing four-hour ceremony. Fans in the stadium and watching on TV around the world were treated to music from stars such as Paul McCartney, a parade of the world's athletes, fireworks galore, and the lighting of the Olympic flame. The show got the Games off to a rousing start.

2012 SUMMER OLYMPICS

Jolly Good Show!

If you love sports, you've GOT to love the Olympic Games. The London Games of 2012 created heroes around the world, and hundreds of memories for fans watching in person and on TV (or online!). A record number of people watched thousands of athletes take part in hundreds of events over 17 amazing days. Fans in London reported that the British people were friendly, helpful, and enthusiastic. And some lucky fans got to hang out with fellow Olympic watchers including soccer star David Beckham, Prince William and his wife, Kate Middleton, or Prince Harry.

Speaking of royalty, was that Queen Elizabeth II skydiving with James Bond into the Opening Ceremony? Well, no, but the Queen's appearance in a video was a highlight of a show that included the creation of an entire English countryside in the stadium, Voldemort battling Mary Poppins, and the lighting of a surprising Olympic torch. Instead of one flame, the London torch was made from 204 copper petals, one for each of the countries taking part. Gathered together, the petals formed a huge fire that glowed throughout the Games.

Once the sports started, the memories were created daily. On fields, in pools, on tracks, on roads, in arenas, on courts, and more . . . sports poured over the country. In London, athletes performed near some of the city's historic buildings. The beach volleyball was held on the Horse Guard Parade. The cycling races and marathon sped by Buckingham Palace. At all the venues, the British people cheered every one of their athletes, whether champions or not, and they racked up the third-most gold medals with a total of 29. The United States, as expected, was the overall medals leader with 104. The big news, though, was that 63 percent of American medals were won by female athletes, the most ever. Gymnast Gabby Douglas, swimmer Missy Franklin, and three-time gold-medal-winning beach volleyball stars Misty May-Treanor and Kerri Walsh Jennings were among the big heroes.

The gold medalists got most of the headlines, but sometimes an Olympic hero was born when an athlete overcame long odds. In diving, China was dominating, but in the men's platform, an American diver pulled a surprise when

__I dreamed about this moment my whole life. I finally got one after 17 years!__

— **MISSY FRANKLIN** AFTER WINNING A GOLD MEDAL

"Golden Gabby" shows off a winning smile, too.

In London, athletes raced past history every day, such as these runners near Big Ben.

David Boudia secured an unexpected gold for the U.S. In judo, no American woman had ever won a medal, but on the second day of the Games, Kayla Harrison did just that. Jennifer Suhr didn't take up pole vaulting until she was 22; she caught up fast, winning gold at the age of 30.

Olympic heroes don't have to be winners, either. Another athlete in judo lasted just 90 seconds in her first and only match. But Wojdan Shaherkani was the first woman ever to compete for Saudi Arabia (see page 30). For more amazing Olympians, see page 27.

From the Queen's jump to the final flame going out on August 12, the London Olympic Games were a celebration of all that is great about sports.

ONE DIRECTION!

Yes, that was popular singing group One Direction starring in the Closing Ceremonies. With the Olympics heading to Rio de Janiero in 2016, the event ended with a big dance tribute to Brazil. (It will be the first time the Olympic Games will be held in South America.) A surprise appearance by soccer superstar Pelé capped things off as the London Olympics came to a close.

American Heroes!

Swim Stars!

The Olympics have been around for more than 100 years, and tens of thousands of athletes have taken part. But none of them did what Michael Phelps did. With six more medals in London, Phelps now has 22 total Olympic medals, 18 of them gold, which is far and away the most ever by a single athlete. He won two different events in three straight Olympics, and

his eight golds in 2008 remain a single-Games mark. You can tell your grandkids you saw the greatest Olympic athlete of all time.

Phelps was not the only U.S. swim star this year, however. Ryan Lochte, Brendan Hansen, and Nathan Adrian, among others, all earned golds. Teenagers Missy Franklin and Katie Ledecky set new records and won gold, too. The U.S. dominated relay events as well, winning three golds.

Bang for the Gold

While Phelps holds the record for most medals, another American Olympian set an all-time mark in London. Kim Rhode won the skeet shooting gold medal, giving her one medal in five straight Olympics. No American Olympian in any sport has ever matched that amazing streak. She was not the only U.S. shooter to bag gold; Vincent Hancock won the men's skeet event.

Golden Girls

Serena Williams stomped the competition to win her first gold medal in singles tennis. She and sister Venus won their third gold in doubles. Serena's singles gold made her the second

Phelps flashed his golden smile four times!

Aly Raisman was a big winner for U.S. gymnastics, earning two golds and a bronze.

woman ever, after Steffi Graf, to win all four Grand Slam events and an Olympic gold medal.

Women on the Move

On the track, the U.S. women's 4x100-meter relay put on an amazing display. The quartet set a new world record while winning the gold medal. Tianna Madison, Allyson Felix, Bianca Knight, and Carmelita Jeter sped around the track in 40.82 seconds. They beat a mark set way back in 1985. For Felix, the race capped off a golden week. She won the 200 meters and also got a relay gold in the 4x400-meter relay.

Jumpin' Gymnasts!

Gabby Douglas became the first American gymnast ever to win both the all-around gold medal as well as the team gold medal. First, she helped her teammates put on an amazing show. Jordyn Wieber, Aly Raisman, Kyla Ross, McKayla Maroney, plus Douglas, narrowly defeated the team from Russia. It was the first American team gold since 1996. Two nights later, Douglas led after every round of the all-around competition. With a great score in the final event, she clinched her gold! Raisman added a gold in the floor exercises, along with a bronze in the balance beam.

Soccer Success!

Perhaps the most dramatic single game at the Olympics was played in soccer by the U.S. and Canadian women's teams. Canada had beaten the U.S. only three times in 51 matches. The U.S. had not lost at the Olympics since 2000. Those records didn't matter to Canada, which held the lead in this semifinal three times, including 3–2 with less than 10 minutes left. However, the U.S. battled back time and again, finally tying the score in the 78th minute. That led to overtime and in the 33rd minute of the extra period, Alex Morgan floated in a header that gave the U.S. a stunning win. They then beat Japan in the gold-medal final, 2–1, to avenge a loss to the Japanese at the 2011 World Cup.

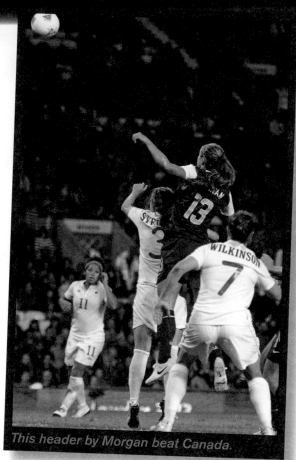

This header by Morgan beat Canada.

James added gold to his 2012 NBA title.

Gee . . . Surprise

The men's and women's basketball teams both came home with gold medals. The men's team boasted 11 NBA All-Stars, including LeBron James, Kobe Bryant, and Chris Paul. They beat Spain in the gold-medal game; Spain featured NBA stars Pau and Marc Gasol, too. The U.S. women's team won its fifth straight gold medal. They haven't lost since 1992, a streak of 41 straight victories. In the gold-medal game, Candace Parker had 21 points as the U.S. defeated France, 86–50.

Amazing Stories

Most people look to the medal stands to find heroes, to see the athletes who captured gold, silver, and bronze. This Olympics, however, boasted heroes of many kinds.

✱ **Oscar Pistorius**, ▶▶▶ a South African runner, became the first athlete to run on artificial legs. His special "Cheetah" blades, coupled with his great athletic ability and drive, earned him a spot in the Games. He made the semifinals of the 400 meters and the finals of the 4x400 relay, but he also made a lot of fans.

✱ You would think that seeing really well is important for an archer. However, **Im Dong-Hyun** of South Korea set a world record in his opening Olympic round, even though he is legally blind. He can see only blurred colors and a few shapes. But he says that actually helps him focus on the target! He focused well enough to win a gold medal, too!

✱ **Natalia Partyka** of Poland didn't let having only one hand stop her from becoming an Olympic table-tennis player. She made it to the round of 32 in her second Olympic Games. She had to learn to flip the ball up for a serve with her elbow, but she earned her place among the world's best—and toughest.

✱ Never too early and never too late for the Games: **Adzo Kpossi**, 13, a swimmer from Togo, was the youngest competitor. The youngest American swimmer was **Katie Ledecky**, and she won a gold medal while setting a world record. At 71, Japan's **Hiroshi Hoketsu** was the oldest. He competed in dressage, a horse-riding event. After the Games, he said he would not be back for another. "My horse is too old now," he said.

✱ Talk about courage: In the middle of his first leg of the men's 4x400 relay, American runner **Manteo Mitchell** heard a crack. His leg burst into pain, "like someone snapped it." But he knew his team was counting on him, so he kept running. After handing off the baton, he fell to the track. He later learned he had run most of the race after breaking a bone in his leg. Wow.

World Stars

Usain Bolt

As a sprinter, nobody does it better . . . and no one ever has. Jamaica's amazing Usain Bolt became the first runner ever to win back-to-back golds in the 100- and 200-meter races at the Olympics. After amazing the world with his first double in 2008, he roared back four years later to double up again. The 100-meter final was the fastest group of all time. It included the runners with the four fastest times ever. But in the end, Usain bolted to the front! He then helped Jamaica set a world record in the 4x100-meter relay.

Chinese Dominate Diving

China was expected to dominate the men's and women's diving events . . . and they sure did. Though an American snuck in with a surprise gold on the second-to-last day, it was otherwise all China at the diving pool. Divers from that country won six of the eight available gold medals, and 10 of the 24 total medals.

Beating the Boss

Kenya has a great reputation for distance running. David Rudisha added another distance to their long list of wins. He set the first world record at Olympic Stadium in the 800 meters. He was the first person to run under 1:41 for the two laps. The first person to run under 1:42? The head of the London Olympic Games, former gold medalist Lord Sebastian Coe.

◀◀◀ O Canada!

Canada captured only one gold medal, by Rosannagh MacLennan in women's trampoline, but it had 18 overall medals. The biggest disappointment came in soccer, where the women's team nearly knocked off the defending-champion American team. A bronze was an unexpected bonus, though. Canadians did very well in water sports, earning medals in kayaking, open-water swimming, diving, swimming, and canoeing.

HOMETOWN HEROES

London was thrilled to put on the Games, and British fans were thrilled by a succession of gold-medal performances by their athletes. Among the host nation's total of 65 medals (29 of them gold) were these highlights:

→ **Andy Murray** became the first British tennis player to be Olympic champ; he beat **Roger Federer** in the final to avenge a loss at Wimbledon (page 163).

→ **Jess Ennis** was proclaimed the best female athlete in the world after winning the difficult seven-event heptathlon. ▶▶▶

→ **Bradley Wiggins** followed up his Tour de France win (page 174) with gold in the time trial. His was one of eight golds won by British cyclists in 18 events.

→ Born in Somalia but raised in England, **Mo Farah** became only the seventh person ever to win both the 5,000- and 10,000-meter runs at the same Olympics.

→ It wasn't gold, but **Zara Phillips** earned silver in the team equestrian event. A bonus: Her mom, **Princess Anne**, presented her with the medal.

WORLD NOTES

◎ **Kirani James** won the first medal ever for the tiny island nation of Grenada, capturing gold in the 400-meter run. Other countries that won first-time medals included Montenegro, Guatemala, Botswana, and Cyprus.

◎ **Katie Taylor** won Ireland's only gold medal of the Games in a new sport: women's boxing.

◎ The BMX final had a repeat men's winner, **Maris Strombergs** of Latvia. Speedy **Marianne Pajon** of Colombia won the women's race.

◎ The 400-meter relay swim team from France got revenge for a 2012 loss, beating **Michael Phelps** and the U.S.

◎ The Bahamas won its only medal of the Games—and first gold by its men ever—with a shocking upset of the U.S. in the 4x400-meter relay. U.S. men had not been beaten in the event since 1952!

Olympic Lists

PHANTASTIC PHELPS

Here's a list of Michael Phelps's record 22 Olympic medals

2012 (London)

EVENT	MEDAL
100 M BUTTERFLY	GOLD
200 M INDIVIDUAL MEDLEY	GOLD
4X200 FREESTYLE RELAY	GOLD
4X100 MEDLEY RELAY	GOLD
200 M BUTTERFLY	SILVER
4X100 FREESTYLE RELAY	SILVER

EVENT	MEDAL
4X100 FREESTYLE RELAY	GOLD
4X200 FREESTYLE RELAY	GOLD
4X100 MEDLEY RELAY	GOLD

2008 (Beijing)

EVENT	MEDAL
100 M BUTTERFLY	GOLD
200 M BUTTERFLY	GOLD
200 M INDIVIDUAL MEDLEY	GOLD
400 M INDIVIDUAL MEDLEY	GOLD

2004 (Athens)

EVENT	MEDAL
100 M BUTTERFLY	GOLD
200 M BUTTERFLY	GOLD
200 M INDIVIDUAL MEDLEY	GOLD
400 M INDIVIDUAL MEDLEY	GOLD
4X200 FREESTYLE RELAY	GOLD
4X100 MEDLEY RELAY	GOLD
200 M FREESTYLE	BRONZE

You Go, Girls!

For the first time in Olympic history, women athletes competed for every nation at the Games. To make it complete, Qatar, Brunei, and Saudi Arabia sent women who competed in track, judo, and shooting. There were also more female athletes in the Games this time than male athletes, including more women than men from the U.S. for the first time. Bonus points to Malaysian shooter Nur Suryani Mohd Taibi, who competed when she was eight months pregnant.

THE MEDAL RACE

Here are the top countries in the medal race from the 2012 Olympic Games.

COUNTRY	GOLD	SILVER	BRONZE	TOTAL
UNITED STATES	46	29	29	**104**
CHINA	38	27	23	**88**
RUSSIA	24	26	32	**82**
GREAT BRITAIN	29	17	19	**65**
GERMANY	11	19	14	**44**
JAPAN	7	14	17	**38**
AUSTRALIA	7	16	12	**35**
FRANCE	11	11	12	**34**
SOUTH KOREA	13	8	7	**28**
ITALY	8	9	11	**28**
NETHERLANDS	6	6	8	**20**
UKRAINE	6	5	9	**20**
CANADA	1	5	12	**18**

NEXT!

The Olympic Games are heading to South America for the first time in 2016. Here's a list of the upcoming Olympic celebrations:

2014	Winter Olympics	**SOCHI, RUSSIA**
2016	Summer Olympics	**RIO DE JANIERO, BRAZIL**
2018	Winter Olympics	**PYEONGCHANG, SOUTH KOREA**
2020	Summer Olympics	**TOKYO, MADRID, OR ISTANBUL***

*Choice to be announced in 2014

NFL

THE PLAY OF THE YEAR!
The Giants did it again! Trailing in the Super Bowl to the Patriots, Eli Manning lofted a perfect pass that Mario Manningham caught right at the sideline. It was the biggest play in a last-minute drive that ended with Ahmad Bradshaw's unusual game-winning touchdown. Why unusual? Turn to page 42 to find out.

The Year of the QB

The season that almost didn't happen turned into one of the most exciting seasons in the past decade. NFL fans had to wait out a long "lockout" in the summer. Team owners and players disagreed on new rules for signing players. The two sides finally agreed in July—much to the relief of fans everywhere!

Once the 2011 season got started, the footballs started flying as never before. By the time the dust settled in January, a stack of new offensive records had been set. More points (11,356) were scored than in any season in NFL history.

One big reason for the high scoring was a pack of powerful passers. **Drew Brees** had 5,476 passing yards, the most ever. **Tom Brady** and **Matthew Stafford** also topped 5,000 yards for the season. In total, NFL QBs had 121 games with 300 or more yards passing, the most ever in one season. Plus, Carolina's **Cam Newton** set records for most passing yards by a rookie while also setting a new mark for rushing touchdowns by *any* QB!

All those passes had to go somewhere. A trio of tight ends emerged in 2011 as huge offensive forces. The Patriots' **Rob Gronkowski** set new records for the position with 17 touchdowns

and 1,327 receiving yards. "Gronk" was also the first TE ever to lead the NFL in TDs. **Jimmy Graham** of the Saints was just behind with 1,310 yards. **Tony Gonzalez** of the Falcons moved to No. 2 all-time in receptions, trailing only the great **Jerry Rice**.

In the Year of the QB, another one of the biggest stories was one passer who didn't play. **Peyton Manning** missed the entire season

Rob Gronkowski set new records for tight ends.

> **❝ If you believe, unbelievable things can sometimes be possible. It's pretty special that we have a team that constantly believes in each other. ❞**
>
> — TIM TEBOW

with a neck injury. The Colts collapsed without him. They finished with a league-worst 2–14 record.

But one QB soared above all the rest in fans' eyes—even though his numbers were puny compared to most passers.

Tim Tebow electrified the NFL with his comeback ability, humble manner, and gutsy running. He took over as the starter in Denver when the team was 1–4 and led them to the division title. Five of the six games he won were by stunning comebacks. Week after week, fans waited for "Tebow Time," as the fourth quarter was called. Some fans didn't like his passing style or his faith-based manner, but everyone agreed: The guy won games.

At the end of the regular season, seven new teams were division champs, including Tebow's Broncos. Only the Patriots repeated from 2010. The playoffs were epic, with comebacks and big plays and stunning surprises. In a season marked by great quarterback play, the Super Bowl came down to the same thing. Which great QB took home the Vince Lombardi Trophy as the NFL champion?

Read on to find out!

Tebow's comeback successes thrilled fans.

2011 Final Regular-Season Standings

AFC EAST	W	L	NFC EAST	W	L
Patriots	13	3	Giants	9	7
Jets	8	8	Eagles	8	8
Dolphins	6	10	Cowboys	8	8
Bills	6	10	Redskins	5	11
AFC NORTH	**W**	**L**	**NFC NORTH**	**W**	**L**
Ravens	12	4	Packers	15	1
Steelers	12	4	Lions	10	6
Bengals	9	7	Bears	8	8
Browns	4	12	Vikings	3	13
AFC SOUTH	**W**	**L**	**NFC SOUTH**	**W**	**L**
Texans	10	6	Saints	13	3
Titans	9	7	Falcons	10	6
Jaguars	5	11	Panthers	6	10
Colts	2	14	Buccaneers	4	12
AFC WEST	**W**	**L**	**NFC WEST**	**W**	**L**
Broncos	8	8	49ers	13	3
Chargers	8	8	Cardinals	8	8
Raiders	8	8	Seahawks	7	9
Chiefs	7	9	Rams	2	14

First Quarter

NFL WEEKS 1–4

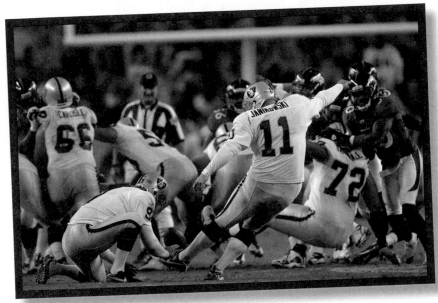

their opener to Houston, kicking off a tough season.

◀◀◀ **✱ Big foot:** Oakland's **Sebastian Janikowski** tied an all-time NFL record with a 63-yard field goal.

✱ Surprise team: The Detroit Lions started out 4–0.

✱ Happy returns 1: In Week 4, the Ravens beat the Jets 34–17. The big news was that there were five scores in the game on returns: two fumbles, two interceptions, and a kickoff.

✱ Good start 1: Carolina QB **Cam Newton** set a rookie record with 422 passing yards in Week 1. Then in Week 2, he broke his own mark!

✱ Good start 2: Meanwhile, **Tom Brady** set a Patriots record with 517 passing yards.

✱ Good start 3: Ted Ginn Jr. scored on a punt return *and* a kickoff return while helping the 49ers win their opener over Seattle.

✱ Bad start: Without their leader, **Peyton Manning**, the Colts lost

✱ Happy returns 2: With a punt-return touchdown against Carolina, Chicago's **Devin Hester** added to his amazing record. He ended 2011 with a record 14 punt-return TDs.

◀◀◀ **✱ Rodgers rolls:** Green Bay's **Aaron Rodgers** got his MVP season rolling with a career-high 408 passing yards in a win over Denver.

Second Quarter
NFL WEEKS 5–8

✱ Sad day: The NFL lost a legendary owner when Oakland's **Al Davis** died in October. Davis had run the Silver and Black since 1963.

✱ Good catch: Future Hall of Fame tight end **Tony Gonzalez** passed Marvin Harrison to take over the No. 2 spot on the all-time receptions list.

✱ Weird win: The Saints lost to the 0–6 Rams in Week 8! That was only the second time in 30 years that the team with the league's worst offense (St. Louis) beat the team with the best offense (New Orleans).

◀◀◀**✱** When the season began, only diehard Dallas fans and perhaps his own family knew who **DeMarco Murray** was. But after injuries knocked out the starts, Murray made the most of his chance for Dallas. In their win over the Rams, Murray ran for a club-record 253 yards.

✱ Never give up: Baltimore trailed Arizona 24–3 in the second quarter in Week 8. No problem: The Ravens scored 27 straight points to rally for a 30–27 win.

✱ It begins: Tebow Time officially began in Week 7. The amazing Denver lefty quarterback led the Broncos to a late-game comeback win over Miami. The Broncos scored 15 points in the fourth quarter and then Tebow led Denver on a game-winning drive in overtime.

◀◀◀**✱ Showdown:** In a matchup of two of the league's hottest teams, the 49ers overcame the Lions 25–19.

Third Quarter

NFL WEEKS 9–12

★ **Tebow Time II:** The hottest player in the NFL created more amazing comebacks. After an easy win over Oakland, **Tebow** ran for the winning score over the Jets in the final minute. Against San Diego, he led drives that led to game-tying and game-winning field goals.

★ **Tough call:** In overtime against the Saints, Falcons head coach **Mike Smith** made a bold move. He went for the first down on fourth-and-inches. Atlanta didn't make it. Big problem: They were on the Saints' 30-yard line. New Orleans kicked a field goal shortly after and won the game.

★ **Wow!:** With a punt return TD against the Rams, Arizona's **Patrick Peterson** became the first player in NFL history with four punt-return TDs of 80 yards or more!

★ Detroit's **Matt Stafford** had a huge day in the Lions' win over Carolina. He threw five touchdown passes. ▶▶▶

◀◀◀ ★ **Passing party:** **Eli Manning** and **Drew Brees** put on a Monday night show. Manning threw for 406 yards. Brees had four TD passes. The Saints won 49–24.

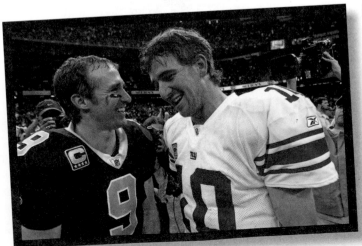

Fourth Quarter
NFL WEEKS 13–17

✱ Rookie record: Cam Newton of the Panthers ended the season with 14 rushing touchdowns, the most ever for a quarterback—rookie or not! ▶▶▶

✱ Here comes Houston: The surprising Texans won their sixth game in a row, defeating Atlanta and earning their first-ever playoff spot.

✱ Tebow Time III: He led Denver to a high-scoring win over the Vikings. Against the Bears, **Tebow** got help from kicker **Matt Prater**. Prater kicked a 59-yarder to tie the game, then Tebow put him in a spot to kick a game-winning 51-yarder in overtime!

✱ Whew!: In Week 15, the Colts beat the Titans to avoid going winless in the season. Indianapolis still ended up with the league's worst record—but they got first pick in the NFL Draft (page 47).

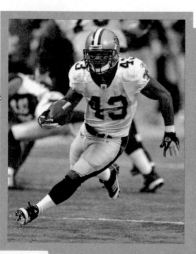

NEW NFL RECORDS!

Along with **Drew Brees**'s new passing marks (page 34), here are some other NFL records set in the 2011 season:

MOST FIELD GOALS: 44, David Akers, 49ers

HIGHEST PASSER RATING: 122.5, Aaron Rodgers, Packers

MOST PASSING YARDS, ROOKIE: 4,051, Cam Newton, Panthers

◀◀◀ **MOST COMBINED YARDS: 2,696**, Darren Sproles, Saints

MOST SEASONS WITH 13-PLUS WINS: 5, Bill Belichick, Patriots

NFL Playoffs

Tebow came through again in the playoffs.

Divisional Championships

AFC **Ravens 20–Texans 13**
The mighty Ravens' D forced key turnovers in Houston's first playoff run. Baltimore picked off **Yates** three times and recovered a fumble.

Patriots 45–Broncos 10
The **Tom Brady** Show ended **Tebow** Time, as the star Patriots QB passed for a playoff-record-tying six touchdowns. Super tight end **Rob Gronkowski** caught three of them, also tying a record.

Wild Card

AFC **Broncos 29–Steelers 23**
Simply amazing: **Tim Tebow** did it again. After Pittsburgh tied the game in the fourth quarter, Tebow threw an 80-yard TD pass on the *first play* of overtime to shock the Steelers.

Texans 31–Bengals 10
Houston won its first-ever playoff game. Star running back **Arian Foster** had two touchdown runs to help out rookie backup QB **T. J. Yates**. The Texans D made three interceptions.

NFC **Giants 24–Falcons 2**
Yes, 2. **Eli Manning** had three touchdown passes, while the Giants defense grounded the Falcons.

Saints 45–Lions 28
Led by **Drew Brees** and his 466 passing yards, the mighty Saints offense blew away the upstart Lions.

Brady jumps for joy after his Patriots dominate Denver to advance.

Davis's catch gave the Niners the win.

NFC **49ers 36–Saints 32**
Alex Smith twice led the Niners to come-from-behind TDs in the final minutes. **Vernon Davis**'s clutch catch in the final minute sealed the deal.

Giants 37–Packers 20
Eli Manning kept rolling with an eye on Indy. He had three touchdown passes, while Green Bay made four turnovers.

Conference Championships

AFC **Patriots 23–Ravens 20**
It was a tough ending for Baltimore as kicker **Billy Cundiff** missed a short field goal that would have tied the game in the final seconds. The win sent New England to its fifth Super Bowl in 11 seasons.

NFC **Giants 20–49ers 17**
It was the opposite ending for the Giants' kicker in this exciting game. **Lawrence Tynes** nailed a 31-yard kick in overtime to send New York to the Super Bowl.

TWO FOR TYNES

When the Giants' **Lawrence Tynes** went onto the field to try for a field goal that would send his team to the Super Bowl . . . everything felt familiar. That's because four years ago, he and the Giants were in the same situation. In that game, they were tied with the Packers, also in overtime. And it was up to Tynes to win the game (or not). In both cases, he came through. "It's my second NFC Championship Game, my second game-winner," Tynes said. "It's amazing. I had dreams about this last night."

Ahmad Bradshaw sat down on the job . . . and in the end zone, giving the Giants the win.

Super Bowl XLVI

Super Bowl XLVI began with a mistake coming out of the end zone and ended with a Giants player backing into the end zone. The matchup was a repeat of the Super Bowl five years ago. Once again,

Wes Welker just missed making a key catch.

the powerful New England Patriots, led by superstar **Tom Brady**, were favored to win. And once again, the surprising New York Giants were helped by an amazing catch late in the game. And just like the last time, the Giants came out on top.

In the first Super Bowl held in Indianapolis, the Giants got on top early. Brady was called for a penalty while standing in his own end zone. That gave the Giants a safety and a 2–0 lead. **Eli Manning** then led a long drive that ended in a touchdown pass to **Victor Cruz**.

But New England battled back. After they got a field goal, the Patriots took the halftime lead after Brady hit **Danny Woodhead** with a short TD pass. The Giants continued to move the ball well against the Patriots, but couldn't crack the end zone. New York scored only a pair of field goals in the third quarter. The Giants got a bit of luck late in the game when **Wes Welker** couldn't hang on to a tough pass from Brady. Welker had led the NFL with 122 receptions, but he couldn't come up with this one. It might have clinched a win for New England.

Instead, Manning and the Giants got the ball back with less than three minutes left and 88 yards to go, down by two points. The play of the game—and the Giants' season—came on a perfect 38-yard pass from Manning to **Mario Manningham**. The receiver tiptoed inbounds and made a spectacular catch. It gave the Giants room to move and a few plays later, they were all the way to the Patriots' six-yard line.

Then came a very strange play. Knowing that time was short and that the Giants would probably score an easy field goal, the Patriots let New York score. Giants running back **Ahmad Bradshaw** actually tried to stop himself as soon as he realized the Patriots' move. He couldn't, though, and backed in for what proved to be the winning score.

The game wasn't over yet. Giants fans had to sweat out a last-play heave to the end zone by Brady. But the ball bounced too far away for **Rob Gronkowski** to snag, and the Giants snagged the Lombardi Trophy. It was the team's fourth Super Bowl victory and eighth NFL championship since they started play in 1925.

THE OTHER BROTHER

While **Peyton Manning** was winning a record four NFL MVP awards, younger brother **Eli** was not getting as much attention. Coming into 2011, he had matched Peyton with a Super Bowl win and a Super Bowl MVP. By the end of the season, Eli had topped Peyton. He won his second Super Bowl MVP award in the win over the Patriots. During the season, he set an NFL record by throwing 15 TD passes in the fourth quarter of games.

BOX SCORE

TEAM	1Q	2Q	3Q	4Q	FINAL
GIANTS	9	0	6	6	21
PATRIOTS	0	10	7	0	17

SCORING

1Q: NYG Safety after Brady penalty in end zone
1Q: NYG Victor Cruz two-yard TD pass from Eli Manning
2Q: NE Stephen Gostkowski 29-yard field goal
2Q: NE Danny Woodhead four-yard TD pass from Tom Brady
3Q: NE Aaron Hernandez 12-yard TD pass from Tom Brady
3Q: NYG Lawrence Tynes 38-yard field goal
3Q: NYG Lawrence Tynes 33-yard field goal
4Q: NYG Ahmad Bradshaw six-yard TD run

2011 Stat Leaders

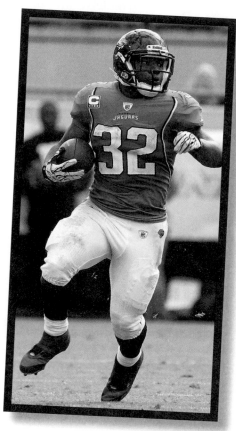

◀◀◀ **1,606** RUSHING YARDS
Maurice Jones-Drew, Jaguars

122.5 PASSER RATING
Aaron Rodgers, Packers

46 TOUCHDOWN PASSES
Drew Brees, Saints

5,476 PASSING YARDS
Drew Brees, Saints

122 RECEPTIONS
Wes Welker, Patriots

1,681 RECEIVING YARDS
Calvin Johnson, Lions

166 POINTS
David Akers, 49ers

22 SACKS ▶▶▶
Jared Allen, Vikings

166 TACKLES
London Fletcher, Redskins

Suggs had 14 sacks and forced 7 fumbles.

NFL HONORS

For the first time, NFL postseason awards were given out on a TV show. The celebrity-packed event aired the night before Super Bowl XLVI.

NFL MVP:
Aaron Rodgers, QB, Packers

DEFENSIVE PLAYER OF THE YEAR:
Terrell Suggs, LB, Ravens

OFFENSIVE PLAYER OF THE YEAR:
Drew Brees, QB, Saints

DEFENSIVE ROOKIE OF THE YEAR:
Von Miller, LB, Broncos

OFFENSIVE ROOKIE OF THE YEAR:
Cam Newton, QB, Panthers

COMEBACK PLAYER OF THE YEAR:
Matt Stafford, QB, Lions

WALTER PAYTON MAN OF THE YEAR:
Matt Birk, C, Ravens

COACH OF THE YEAR:
Jim Harbaugh, 49ers

PLAY OF THE YEAR

The 2011 NFL season was only a few seconds old when Packers rookie **Randall Cobb** carried the season's opening kickoff back 108 yards for a touchdown. By the time the season was over, nothing had topped that remarkable return. NFL fans voted Cobb's record-tying runback as the NFL Play of the Year.

Hall of Fame 2012

Here are the men who joined the ranks of the immortals in the Pro Football Hall of Fame in August 2012.

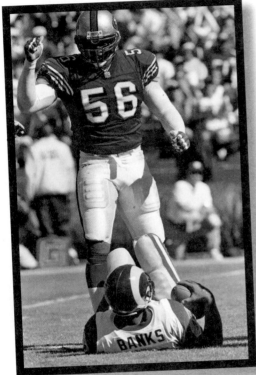

Jack Butler

Steelers defensive back who was No. 2 all-time with 52 interceptions when he retired in 1959

Dermontti Dawson

Awesome Steelers center who helped team win Super Bowl XL

◀◀◀Chris Doleman

Powerful defensive end who racked up 150 sacks; played for Vikings, 49ers, and Falcons

Cortez Kennedy

Seattle defensive tackle who was a run-stopping force

Curtis Martin ▶▶▶

Fourth all-time with 14,101 rushing yards; played for Jets and Patriots

Willie Roaf

Powerful Saints tackle who made 11 Pro Bowl teams

NFL Draft Top 10

The first pick was no surprise, but the rest? That got very interesting.

PICK	PLAYER/SCHOOL	NFL TEAM
1	**Andrew LUCK**, QB	Colts ▶▶▶
2	**Robert GRIFFIN III**, QB	Redskins
3	**Trent RICHARDSON**, RB	Browns
4	**Matt KALIL**, OT	Vikings
5	**Justin BLACKMON**, WR	Jaguars
6	**Morris CLAIBORNE**, DB	Cowboys
7	**Mark BARRON**, S	Buccaneers
8	**Ryan TANNEHILL**, QB	Dolphins
9	**Luke KUECHLY**, ILB	Panthers
10	**Stephon GILMORE**, DB	Bills

THE FOOTBALL NORTH

The Canadian Football League doesn't get nearly as much attention as the NFL. Fans all over Canada, however, cheered in 2011 when an all-football record fell.

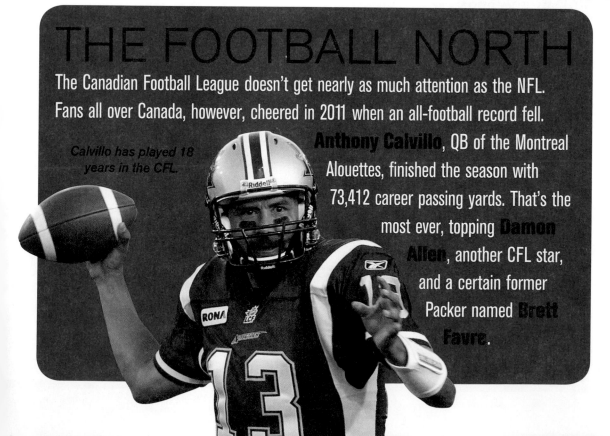

Calvillo has played 18 years in the CFL.

Anthony Calvillo, QB of the Montreal Alouettes, finished the season with 73,412 career passing yards. That's the most ever, topping **Damon Allen**, another CFL star, and a certain former Packer named **Brett Favre**.

For the Record

Super Bowl Winners

GAME	SEASON	WINNING TEAM	LOSING TEAM	SCORE	SITE
XLVI	2011	**N.Y. Giants**	New England	**21-17**	Indianapolis
XLV	2010	**Green Bay**	Pittsburgh	**31-25**	Dallas
XLIV	2009	**New Orleans**	Indianapolis	**31-17**	South Florida
XLIII	2008	**Pittsburgh**	Arizona	**27-23**	Tampa
XLII	2007	**N.Y. Giants**	New England	**17-14**	Glendale, Ariz.
XLI	2006	**Indianapolis**	Chicago	**29-17**	South Florida
XL	2005	**Pittsburgh**	Seattle	**21-10**	Detroit
XXXIX	2004	**New England**	Philadelphia	**24-21**	Jacksonville
XXXVIII	2003	**New England**	Carolina	**32-29**	Houston
XXXVII	2002	**Tampa Bay**	Oakland	**48-21**	San Diego
XXXVI	2001	**New England**	St. Louis	**20-17**	New Orleans
XXXV	2000	**Baltimore**	N.Y. Giants	**34-7**	Tampa
XXXIV	1999	**St. Louis**	Tennessee	**23-16**	Atlanta
XXXIII	1998	**Denver**	Atlanta	**34-19**	South Florida
XXXII	1997	**Denver**	Green Bay	**31-24**	San Diego
XXXI	1996	**Green Bay**	New England	**35-21**	New Orleans
XXX	1995	**Dallas**	Pittsburgh	**27-17**	Tempe, Ariz.
XXIX	1994	**San Francisco**	San Diego	**49-26**	South Florida
XXVIII	1993	**Dallas**	Buffalo	**30-13**	Atlanta
XXVII	1992	**Dallas**	Buffalo	**52-17**	Pasadena
XXVI	1991	**Washington**	Buffalo	**37-24**	Minneapolis

GAME	SEASON	WINNING TEAM	LOSING TEAM	SCORE	SITE
XXV	1990	N.Y. Giants	Buffalo	20–19	Tampa
XXIV	1989	San Francisco	Denver	55–10	New Orleans
XXIII	1988	San Francisco	Cincinnati	20–16	South Florida
XXII	1987	Washington	Denver	42–10	San Diego
XXI	1986	N.Y. Giants	Denver	39–20	Pasadena
XX	1985	Chicago	New England	46–10	New Orleans
XIX	1984	San Francisco	Miami	38–16	Stanford
XVIII	1983	L.A. Raiders	Washington	38–9	Tampa
XVII	1982	Washington	Miami	27–17	Pasadena
XVI	1981	San Francisco	Cincinnati	26–21	Pontiac, Mich.
XV	1980	Oakland	Philadelphia	27–10	New Orleans
XIV	1979	Pittsburgh	Los Angeles	31–19	Pasadena
XIII	1978	Pittsburgh	Dallas	35–31	Miami
XII	1977	Dallas	Denver	27–10	New Orleans
XI	1976	Oakland	Minnesota	32–14	Pasadena
X	1975	Pittsburgh	Dallas	21–17	Miami
IX	1974	Pittsburgh	Minnesota	16–6	New Orleans
VIII	1973	Miami	Minnesota	24–7	Houston
VII	1972	Miami	Washington	14–7	Los Angeles
VI	1971	Dallas	Miami	24–3	New Orleans
V	1970	Baltimore	Dallas	16–13	Miami
IV	1969	Kansas City	Minnesota	23–7	New Orleans
III	1968	N.Y. Jets	Baltimore	16–7	Miami
II	1967	Green Bay	Oakland	33–14	Miami
I	1966	Green Bay	Kansas City	35–10	Los Angeles

CRIMSON DIVE

*On the way to winning the 2011
BCS National Championship, Alabama
had to battle through the tough Southeastern
Conference. Quarterback A. J. McCarron gave his all to
score this touchdown against SEC rival Tennessee. Alabama
won the eighth national championship for the SEC since the BCS
started in 1998. Who won the first? That's right: Tennessee.*

COLLEGE FOOTBALL

Who's No.1?

The 2011 college football season was like a game of king of the mountain. Louisiana State University (LSU) started out on top. For the next four months, teams from all over the country tried to knock them off.

LSU kicked off the season by shutting down the powerful Oregon offense. The Ducks had played for the national title the year before, but LSU's defense proved too powerful and the Tigers won 40–27. The LSU D then allowed only 11 or fewer points in nine of their next 10 games!

Alabama came close to beating LSU in what some fans boldly called The Game of the Century. The game on November 5 matched the two best defenses in the country, and neither team scored a touchdown. The difference, though, was that Alabama missed four field goals. The game went into overtime and LSU won 9–6.

For the next month, a series of top teams tried to reach the No. 2 spot that would give them a final chance against LSU, which kept rolling toward a spot in the Bowl Championship Series (BCS) title game. Oklahoma State had a very strong offense, but fell off the mountain after being upset by Iowa State. Boise State and TCU both had a shot, but lost in upsets.

Oregon (green) gave mighty LSU an early-season challenge.

Stanford star Andrew Luck led the Cardinal.

FINAL 2011 TOP 10
Final Associated Press Poll

1. **Alabama**
2. **LSU**
3. **Oklahoma State**
4. **Oregon**
5. **Arkansas**
6. **USC**
7. **Stanford**
8. **Boise State**
9. **South Carolina**
10. **Wisconsin**

QB Brandon Weeden led the OSU offense.

Out West, Stanford, behind ace QB Andrew Luck, was undefeated . . . until they ran into the Oregon buzzsaw. The Ducks had bounced back from their season-opening loss to LSU and hadn't lost since. That is, they hadn't lost until they, too, fell off the mountain by losing to USC.

Arkansas tried to sneak into the picture. LSU put a stop to that with a 41–17 stomping of the Razorbacks.

For a trip to the BCS title game, that left only Georgia to overcome in the SEC Championship Game. The Bulldogs proved no match, either, and LSU headed toward a date with the No. 2 team after a 42–10 win.

Who would be that No. 2 team? It all came down to the computers. To determine the No. 1 and No. 2 teams, coaches' and sportswriters' votes are combined with computer analysis. When the numbers were all crunched, Alabama squeaked into the final by just 0.0086 points over Oklahoma State. It was the first rematch in 14 years of BCS Championship Games. That rematch, however, gave us a new king on top of the mountain. Check out page 55 for the story!

MORE CHANGES IN 2012

The college football merry-go-round keeps spinning. Once again in 2012, several schools jump from conference to conference. Here are the biggest changes:

BIG EAST: Adds five schools: Central Florida, Houston, SMU, Boise State, and San Diego State. Drops West Virginia, Pitt, and Syracuse.

BIG 12: Drops to nine schools as Missouri moves to the SEC.

SEC: Adds Missouri and Texas A&M.

2011 BCS Bowl Games

Discover Orange Bowl

West Virginia 70, Clemson 33
WVU's Geno Smith tied a bowl record with six touchdown passes.

Allstate Sugar Bowl

Michigan 23, Virginia Tech 20
An overtime field goal was the difference for the Wolverines.

Tostitos Fiesta Bowl

Oklahoma State 41, Stanford 38
Stanford missed two field goals, including one in overtime. Ouch!

◄◄◄ Rose Bowl

Oregon 45, Wisconsin 38
The Ducks quacked last in this offense-oriented game; it was their first Rose Bowl win in 95 years!

OTHER DIVISION CHAMPS

Football Championship Subdivision
North Dakota St. 17, Sam Houston St. 6

Division II
Pittsburg St. 35, Wayne St. 21 ▶▶▶

Division III
Wisc.-Whitewater 13, Mount Union 10

'BAMA WINS THE REMATCH

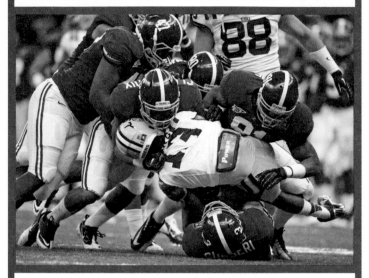

The 2011 championship game was a repeat. LSU had already beaten Alabama 9–6 earlier in the season in a defense-oriented battle of field goals. Many fans wanted to see Oklahoma State take on the undefeated Tigers instead of Alabama.

The Crimson Tide, however, proved they belonged . . . and more. Showing off their tremendous defense, Alabama posted the first shutout in BCS Championship Game history, blanking LSU 21–0. LSU's defense proved pretty powerful, too, keeping Alabama out of the end zone until the fourth quarter. But 'Bama kicker **Jeremy Shelley** was on the money, making five field goals. Meanwhile, LSU could not move the ball past midfield until late in the game. In fact, Alabama outgained LSU 384 yards to 92 yards!

It was the eighth national championship for Alabama. The win also gave the Southeastern Conference its eighth BCS championship, including the last six in a row. To win the national college football title, it seems, you first have to head south.

Points Explosion!

It was not a BCS bowl, but the 2011 Alamo Bowl was one of the most exciting games of the year. The defenses for Baylor and Washington must have missed the trip. It seemed like each team scored whenever it got the ball. Baylor's **Terrance Ganaway** ran for five touchdowns, while Washington QB **Keith Price** threw for four. The teams combined for 1,397 yards. When the dust settled, it was the highest-scoring non-overtime bowl game ever: Baylor 67, Washington 56!

Wow!

Stories from a great year in college football

Fantastic Finishes

Wisconsin was ranked number six and had its eye on a national title when they played Michigan State on October 22. The game was tied with just a few seconds left. There was time for one more play . . . and MSU made it count. On a play called "Rocket," receiver **Keith Nichol** caught a 44-yard pass that bounced off a teammate's facemask. He then squeaked into the end zone to give his team a miracle win.

To make matters worse for Wisconsin, they gave up another game-winner the next week. Ohio State completed a 40-yard Hail Mary pass to send the Badgers to another painful defeat.

Another big game ended in overtime when No. 3 Oklahoma State lost to Iowa State. Iowa State intercepted a pass by OSU's **Brandon Weeden**. A few plays later, **Jeff Woody** scored on a short run. The crowd poured onto the field in celebration!

Nichol (front) after his amazing catch.

Pretty Keenum! ▶

Houston's **Case Keenum** is no stranger to big numbers. He led the NCAA in passing yards in 2010 and 2011. But a game in October added more records to his list. In leading Houston to a 73–34 win over Rice, he threw a record nine TD passes. That also made him the career leader in that category, after becoming the total offense leader a week earlier.

Almost Upsets

Utah State almost had a stunning upset of defending national champion Auburn. In the opening game of the season, Utah State led by 10 points late. However, the Tigers showed why they were the 2010 champs. They scored two touchdowns in the final two minutes and roared back to win 42–38. . . . Up by 20 points as the fourth quarter began, Maryland suddenly unraveled. They let North Carolina State score five TDs in the final quarter. NC State ended up winning handily, 56–41. The shocking loss capped off a tough year for the Terrapins, who lost their last eight games.

Oops!

Missed field goals played a big part in many key games in 2011.

➤ Alabama missed four field goals in their 9–6 loss to LSU.

➤ Boise State's perfect record was ruined with a loss to TCU that hinged on a miss.

➤ Oklahoma State probably missed out on a shot at the BCS title game by missing and losing to Iowa State.

➤ Oregon saw its national title hopes dim by missing a tying field goal against USC.

TCU players watched a Boise State miss give them a win.

Big Night in the Big House

Fans set a record on September 10 when they filled every one of the 114,804 seats at enormous Michigan Stadium, known as the "Big House." They were there for the first night game ever played in the 84-year-old building and everyone wanted to see great action. They got their wish.

Visiting Notre Dame led the home team 24–7 after three quarters. The Wolverines' star QB **Denard Robinson** led a furious comeback. Michigan scored three touchdowns to take the lead. Notre Dame answered, going ahead 31–28. But Robinson still had a little time. As the fans cheered him on, he drove Michigan down the field and threw a 16-yard TD pass to **Roy Roundtree** with just two seconds left. It was the third season in a row that Michigan had stunned Notre Dame with a last-minute win.

◀ Two for the Trophy

On his way to the Heisman Trophy (page 61) Baylor's **Robert Griffin III** had two memorable games.

➤ In the season opener, Baylor gave up a 24-point lead but rallied back to upset TCU. Griffin threw for 359 yards and five touchdowns against one of the best defenses in the country.

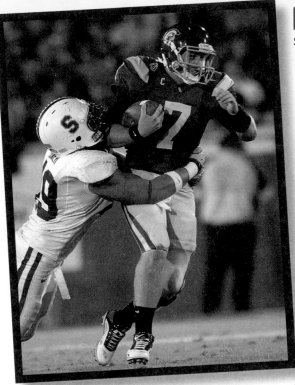

Mr. Everything

Stanford fans enjoyed watching **Andrew Luck** pass and run their team into national-title contention. They'll miss him now that he's jumped to the NFL. In a game against UCLA, Luck added another job: receiver. On a trick play, he flared down the sideline. The pass from **Drew Terrell** was wobbly, but Luck made an amazing one-handed grab for the first down! Here's guessing he won't be catching any passes for the Indianapolis Colts in 2012!

◀ Game of the Year?

What many fans called the most exiting game of the year didn't want to end. It was an epic battle between two great offenses, led by Luck and USC's **Matt Barkley**.

Regular time ended 34–34. Overtime was thrilling, with each team scoring on their first two possessions. Stanford made it three in a row. USC then got its shot to match and made it to the four-yard line. But then **Curtis McNeal** fumbled the ball, Stanford recovered, and the game was finally over: Stanford 56, USC 48.

➤ Facing Oklahoma and trailing late, Griffin led an 80-yard drive in less than a minute. It ended with Griffin's game-winning touchdown pass. The game also included an 87-yard TD pass to **Kendall Wright**.

HIGH SCHOOL BONUS

The Aledo (Texas) High team will miss **Johnathan Gray** in 2012. He wrapped up a record-breaking high school year by scoring his 205th career touchdown while helping his team win its third straight state title. He had 70 touchdowns in 2011 alone! He carries on his football career at the University of Texas in 2012.

Stat City!

FBS leaders in key stat categories

1,923 RUSHING YARDS
Montee BALL, Wisconsin ▶▶▶

33 RUSHING TDS
Montee BALL, Wisconsin ▶▶▶

5,631 PASSING YARDS
Case KEENUM, Houston

48 PASSING TDS
Case KEENUM, Houston

140 RECEPTIONS
Jordan WHITE, Western Michigan

20 TD CATCHES
◀◀◀ **Patrick EDWARDS**, Houston

29 FIELD GOALS
Randy BULLOCK, Texas A&M

191 TACKLES
Luke KUECHLY, Boston College

Conference Champs

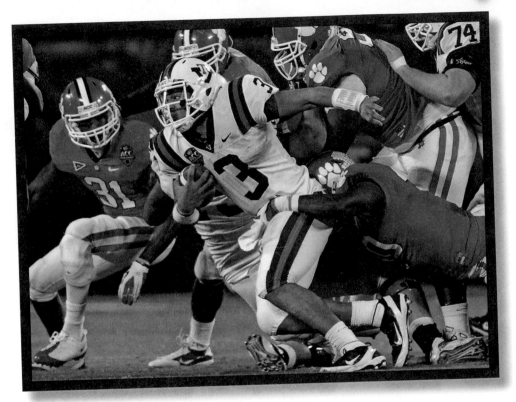

ATLANTIC COAST ▲

Clemson surprised many experts by winning the Atlantic Division and posting a 10–3 overall record. They met Virginia Tech, champs of the Coastal Division, in the conference championship game. The Tigers had beaten the Hokies earlier . . . and they did it again in the title game, winning 38–10.

BIG EAST

A last-play field goal gave West Virginia five wins and a share of the Big East title with Cincinnati and Louisville. The Mountaineers were ranked highest nationally among the three, so they got the Orange Bowl bid.

BIG TEN

It's got 12 teams now, but it's still the Big Ten! Wisconsin was the class of the conference and earned a Rose Bowl berth by defeating Michigan State in the first Big Ten Championship game. Their 42–39 victory avenged a stunning earlier loss to the Spartans (see page 56).

BIG 12

This conference has just 10 teams, but kept its name: Big 12. They lost Nebraska and Colorado, and they also got rid of their championship game. Oklahoma State ended up with the best Big 12 record, as its high-scoring offense helped them go 8–1 in the conference. At 12–1 overall, they ended up No. 3 nationally.

PAC-12 ▶▶▶

In the first-ever Pac-12 Championship Game, Oregon beat UCLA to earn its first Rose Bowl berth since 1995. The Bruins made the Pac-12 title game because USC was banned from bowl games for the year . . . the week before, USC beat UCLA 50–0!

SOUTHEASTERN

For the first time, the national champion didn't even win its own conference. LSU finished ahead of eventual champ Alabama in the East Division and earned a spot in the conference championship game. They faced Georgia, winners of the West Division. LSU defeated Georgia 42–10 as all-around star Tyrann "Honey Badger" Mathieu recovered a fumble, returned a punt for a TD, plus carried back another punt to set up a score.

RG 3 Is No. 1

With a late surge of success, high-scoring quarterback **Robert Griffin III** won the Heisman Trophy as the best college player in the country. RG3, as he's known, then chose to head off to the NFL. Baylor fans will miss him, but he created a lot of great memories.

Griffin set a new single-season passing efficiency record of 192.3, while throwing 37 touchdown passes. He was the first player from Baylor to win the award. He also ran for 644 yards and nine touchdowns.

Finishing second for the second year in a row was Andrew Luck, the superstar Stanford quarterback. It was the third year in a row a Stanford player was the runner-up.

We're No.1!

These are the teams that have finished at the top of the Associated Press's final rankings since the poll was first introduced in 1936.

SEASON	TEAM	RECORD	SEASON	TEAM	RECORD
2011	Alabama	12–1	1973	Notre Dame	11–0
2010	Auburn	14–0	1972	USC	12–0
2009	Alabama	14–0	1971	Nebraska	13–0
2008	Florida	13–1	1970	Nebraska	11–0–1
2007	LSU	12–2	1969	Texas	11–0
2006	Florida	13–1	1968	Ohio State	10–0
2005	Texas	13–0	1967	USC	10–1
2004	USC	13–0	1966	Notre Dame	9–0–1
2003	USC	12–1	1965	Alabama	9–1–1
2002	Ohio State	14–0	1964	Alabama	10–1
2001	Miami	12–0	1963	Texas	11–0
2000	Oklahoma	13–0	1962	USC	11–0
1999	Florida State	12–0	1961	Alabama	11–0
1998	Tennessee	13–0	1960	Minnesota	8–2
1997	Michigan	12–0	1959	Syracuse	11–0
1996	Florida	12–1	1958	LSU	11–0
1995	Nebraska	12–0	1957	Auburn	10–0
1994	Nebraska	13–0	1956	Oklahoma	10–0
1993	Florida State	12–1	1955	Oklahoma	11–0
1992	Alabama	13–0	1954	Ohio State	10–0
1991	Miami	12–0	1953	Maryland	10–1
1990	Colorado	11–1–1	1952	Michigan State	9–0
1989	Miami	11–1	1951	Tennessee	10–1
1988	Notre Dame	12–0	1950	Oklahoma	10–1
1987	Miami	12–0	1949	Notre Dame	10–0
1986	Penn State	12–0	1948	Michigan	9–0
1985	Oklahoma	11–1	1947	Notre Dame	9–0
1984	Brigham Young	13–0	1946	Notre Dame	8–0–1
1983	Miami	11–1	1945	Army	9–0
1982	Penn State	11–1	1944	Army	9–0
1981	Clemson	12–0	1943	Notre Dame	9–1
1980	Georgia	12–0	1942	Ohio State	9–1
1979	Alabama	12–0	1941	Minnesota	8–0
1978	Alabama	11–1	1940	Minnesota	8–0
1977	Notre Dame	11–1	1939	Texas A&M	11–0
1976	Pittsburgh	12–0	1938	Texas Christian	11–0
1975	Oklahoma	11–1	1937	Pittsburgh	9–0–1
1974	Oklahoma	11–0	1936	Minnesota	7–1

BOWL CHAMPIONSHIP SERIES
NATIONAL CHAMPIONSHIP GAMES

College football (at its highest level) is one of the few sports that doesn't have an on-field play-off to determine its champion. In the 1998 season, the NCAA introduced the Bowl Championship Series (BCS), which pits the top two teams in the title game according to a complicated formula that takes into account records, polls, and computer rankings. At the end of the regular season, the No. 1 and No. 2 teams meet in a championship game.

SEASON	SCORE	SITE
2011	**Alabama 21, LSU 0**	NEW ORLEANS, LA
2010	**Auburn 22, Oregon 19**	GLENDALE, AZ
2009	**Alabama 37, Texas 21**	PASADENA, CA
2008	**Florida 24, Oklahoma 14**	MIAMI, FL
2007	**LSU 38, Ohio State 24**	NEW ORLEANS, LA
2006	**Florida 41, Ohio State 14**	GLENDALE, AZ
2005	**Texas 41, USC 38**	PASADENA, CA
2004	**USC 55, Oklahoma 19**	MIAMI, FL
2003	**LSU 21, Oklahoma 14**	NEW ORLEANS, LA
2002	**Ohio State 31, Miami 24**	TEMPE, AZ
2001	**Miami 37, Nebraska 14**	PASADENA, CA
2000	**Oklahoma 13, Florida State 2**	MIAMI, FL
1999	**Florida State 46, Virginia Tech 29**	NEW ORLEANS, LA
1998	**Tennessee 23, Florida State 16**	TEMPE, AZ

FREESE FRAME
In one of the biggest moments of one of the best World Series in recent years, David Freese of the Cardinals danced home with the winning run in Game 6. Freese's walk-off homer capped off St. Louis's second comeback against the Rangers. The Cardinals ended up winning the 2011 championship in seven memorable games. Read more about it on page 70.

MLB

What a Night!

Evan Longoria's walk-off homer sent the Rays to the playoffs.

The Yankees Hall of Fame catcher **Yogi Berra** once said, "It ain't over till it's over." That was never more true than in the 2011 Major League Baseball season. That year ended with one of the most surprising final days in the sport's long history. (Then the World Series almost lived up to the excitement of late September; see page 70.)

In early September, the Red Sox and Braves looked like locks for the playoffs. Both were up by at least 8.5 games. By the end of the month, however, the Rays and the Cardinals had rocketed upward. On September 28, the final day of the season, four games were played at almost the same time—and all of them affected the playoffs. Fans jumped from TV to the Internet to radio trying to follow the pitch-by-pitch action. Here's what happened:

In the National League, the night began with the Braves tied for the wild-card spot with the Cardinals. St. Louis took care of business, beating the Astros, 8–0. However, the Braves choked. With Atlanta up by a run in the top of the ninth over the Phillies, All-Star closer **Craig Kimbrel** let in the tying run. Four extra innings later, the Phillies' **Hunter Pence** drove in the winning run. The shocking loss sent the Braves home for the winter.

As the Braves game was ending, the drama in the American League was continuing. The Red Sox and Rays tied for the wild-card spot in the AL. Playing Baltimore, the Sox built up a 3–2 lead heading to the ninth.

Meanwhile, in Florida, Tampa Bay was playing the Yankees and getting crushed. The Rays trailed 7–0 in the eighth inning. But this team had come back from nine games back to tie Boston. They weren't giving up. Down by seven runs to the Yanks, they scored six in the eighth, three coming on **Evan Longoria**'s homer. In the bottom of the ninth, down to their last strike, Tampa players went crazy as pinch-hitter **Dan Johnson**'s homer tied the score.

With Boston still ahead, the Rays needed a miracle.

They got one: The Red Sox bullpen collapsed. In the bottom of the ninth

"*The most shocking, unbelievable, thrilling night in baseball history!*"
— ESPN.COM

inning, after tying the score, Baltimore's **Robert Andino** slapped a pitch from **Jonathan Papelbon** into left field. **Carl Crawford** tried to make a diving catch . . . and he missed. The ball landed safely, a run scored from second, and the Orioles won the game.

Three minutes later, Longoria hit a walk-off homer in the bottom of the 12th inning and the Rays won!

The collapses by Boston and Atlanta were the biggest in baseball history. It was truly a night to remember.

Other highlights of the 2011 season included the stunning success of **Justin Verlander**. The Tigers' righthander became the first pitcher since 1992 to win the Cy Young Award and Most Valuable Player in the same season.

Baseball has been played for more than 150 years, but as 2011 showed, it just keeps getting better!

stin Verlander minated AL ters in 2011.

2011 FINAL STANDINGS

AL EAST
Yankees	97–65
Rays	91–71
Red Sox	90–72
Blue Jays	81–81
Orioles	69–93

AL CENTRAL
Tigers	95–67
Indians	80–82
White Sox	79–83
Royals	71–91
Twins	63–99

AL WEST
Rangers	96–66
Angels	86–76
Athletics	74–88
Mariners	67–95

NL EAST
Phillies	102–60
Braves	89–73
Nationals	80–81
Mets	77–85
Marlins	72–90

NL CENTRAL
Brewers	96–66
Cardinals	90–72
Reds	79–83
Pirates	72–90
Cubs	71–91
Astros	56–106

NL WEST
Diamondbacks	94–68
Giants	86–76
Dodgers	82–79
Rockies	73–89
Padres	71–91

2011 Division Series

AMERICAN LEAGUE
Texas 3, Tampa Bay 1

Tampa won Game 1, 9–0, behind two homers by **Kelly Shoppach**. The Rays knocked Texas ace **C. J. Wilson** out early. In Game 2, Texas put together a five-run fourth inning, and **Mitch Moreland** added a late clinching homer. A big inning gave the Rangers the win in Game 3, too; they scored all four of their runs in the seventh. **Adrian Beltre** belted three homers in Game 4 to help the Rangers win, 4–3, and advance to the ALCS again.

NATIONAL LEAGUE
Cardinals 3, Phillies 2

Ace **Roy Halladay** got a lot of help as the Phillies won Game 1, 11–6. St. Louis tied the series with a four-run Game 2 comeback. In Game 3, the Phils got the winning runs on a pinch-hit homer by **Ben Francisco**. In Game 4, **David Freese** began his amazing postseason (see page 71) with four RBI in a Cardinals win. Game 5 was a classic— Halladay vs. Cards' star **Chris Carpenter**. Both pitched beautifully, but St. Louis won the game, 1–0, and the series.

Tigers 3, Yankees 2

After **Robinson Cano** pounded six RBI, including a grand slam, to lead the Yanks to a 9–3 win in Game 1, it looked like another playoff title for New York. But the Tigers battled back, winning Game 2 behind **Max Scherzer**. In Game 3, AL MVP **Justin Verlander** gave Detroit eight strong innings and they won, 5–4. The Yankees evened the series with a 10–1 rout. Game 5 was set for New York City. The visiting Tigers pulled a surprise. Their bullpen held off the Bronx Bombers, and Detroit won, 3–2.

Brewers 3, Diamondbacks 2

Pitcher **Yovani Gallardo** guided Milwaukee to a Game 1 win, while a five-run sixth helped them win Game 2. The D-backs came back to win Game 3, helped by **Paul Goldschmidt**'s grand slam. In Game 4, Arizona crushed four homers and won again. The deciding Game 5 went to the 10th inning. That's when Milwaukee's **Nyjer Morgan** hit a walk-off single that scored the winning run.

The Tigers celebrated their upset of the Yankees.

2011 Championship Series

AMERICAN LEAGUE
Texas 4, Detroit 2

Texas expected to be here. Detroit was still a bit surprised. The Rangers' bullpen outlasted two rain delays to secure a win in Game 1. Game 2 saw one of the most memorable sights in recent years: Texas outfielder **Nelson Cruz**'s stunning grand slam. It was the first walk-off grand slam in MLB postseason history. Three homers and a great job by pitcher **Doug Fister** helped Detroit bounce back in Game 3. Cruz hit another late homer, this one a three-run shot in the 11th, to give Texas another win. The stubborn Tigers won Game 5. Detroit's solid season came to an end in Game 6. Continuing his record-setting power surge, Cruz hit his sixth homer in the Series and Texas won big, 15–5.

Cruz celebrates his awesome grand slam.

Braun led the Brewers in the NLCS.

NATIONAL LEAGUE
Cardinals 4, Brewers 2

Four RBI from NL MVP **Ryan Braun** powered Milwaukee to a Game 1 win. Superstar **Albert Pujols** drove in five of the Cardinals' 12 runs in their Game 2 win. A fast start by St. Louis in Game 3 gave ace **Chris Carpenter** all he needed to win. Great baserunning was the key to Milwaukee's Game 4 win to even the series. Stolen bases put Brewers in position to score the winning runs. Cardinals bats put up seven runs in Game 5, while the team's bullpen was outstanding. In the clinching Game 6, it was never close. **Freese** had three more RBI and St. Louis capped off an amazing comeback (see page 66) for its 18th NL pennant.

2011 World Series

It's not called the "Fall Classic" for nothing. After the remarkable end to the regular season, the postseason kept the action hot. When the dust settled after this World Series, some fans were calling it one of the best ever played. Here's how it all happened.

GAME 1 Cardinals 3, Rangers 2
St. Louis sent its ace **Chris Carpenter** to the mound in front of a sea of fans wearing red. Carpenter pitched six strong innings. The team took him out for a pinch-hitter, **Allen Craig**, who promptly hit an RBI single that gave St. Louis the lead for good.

GAME 2 Rangers 2, Cardinals 1
Another pinch-hit RBI by Craig gave the Cardinals a 1–0 lead, which they carried into the ninth. That's when the Rangers got

Pujols made history with his bat in Game 3.

hot. They scored two runs off Cards closer **Jason Motte** and held on to win. It was the first time since the 1985 Series that a team trailing, 1–0, in the ninth came back to win.

GAME 3 Cardinals 16, Rangers 7
If pitching was the story of the first two games, hitting took over in Game 3. **Albert Pujols** put on one of the most impressive shows in Series history. Tying a record held by **Babe Ruth** and **Reggie Jackson**, Pujols hit three homers in the game. He had six RBI and 14 total bases in the game.

GAME 4 Rangers 4, Cardinals 0
In 2011, **Derek Holland** pitched for the Rangers, but in one playoff game, he walked batter after batter and had to trudge away disappointed. In this game, he walked away a winner. Holland silenced Pujols and the Cardinals bats, allowing only two hits and two walks in 8 1/3 shutout innings. His catcher, **Mike Napoli**, backed him up with a three-run homer.

Napoli's homer won Game 4 for Texas.

St. Louis won its 11th World Series, the most by a team from the NL.

GAME 5
Rangers 4, Cardinals 2

Game 5 was tied, 2–2, until the bottom of the eighth. That's when Napoli came through again. He hit a two-run double to give the Rangers the lead. Closer **Neftali Feliz** shut down the Cards in the ninth.

GAME 6 Cardinals 10, Rangers 9

Hold on to your hats: This one was awesome! The Cardinals and Rangers played what was called an instant classic. St. Louis came back again and again, with surprise star **David Freese** in the middle of all of it. Twice they were down to their last strike, only to rally again. The Rangers were on top, 7–5, thanks to homers from Cruz and Beltre. Then the Cardinals scored two runs in the bottom of the ninth to tie the game. Freese hit a two-run triple over Cruz's head in right with two outs. A homer by Texas slugger **Josh Hamilton** gave the Rangers the lead in the 10th. But another St. Louis rally tied the score again. Finally, Freese led off the bottom of the 11th with a walk-off homer!

GAME 7 Cardinals 6, Rangers 2

After all the homers and all the drama, it was only right that this Series got a Game 7. The Cardinals proved to have more heroes than the Rangers, though. Carpenter pitched another gem. Freese came through with two more RBI, and Craig hit his third homer of the Series. The Cardinals' inspiring season ended with a happy dance on the infield in front of the home crowd.

FREESE GOT HOT

Outfielder **David Freese** came into the 2011 World Series well-known to family, friends, and a few Cardinals fans. When he finished, he was the talk of baseball. In the playoffs and the Series, Freese came through time and again. His walk-off homer in Game 6 will be part of Series legend. His 21 RBI in the postseason is a new record. But Freese's story is almost as amazing. He was cut by the Padres, had some legal trouble, and then took off with the Cardinals—his hometown team!

2011 Award Winners

MOST VALUABLE PLAYER
AL: **Justin Verlander**
TIGERS
NL: **Ryan Braun**
BREWERS

CY YOUNG AWARD
AL: **Justin Verlander**
TIGERS
NL: **Clayton Kershaw** ▶▶▶
DODGERS

ROOKIE OF THE YEAR
AL: **Jeremy Hellickson**
RAYS
NL: **Craig Kimbrel**
BRAVES

COMEBACK PLAYER OF THE YEAR
AL: **Jacoby Ellsbury**
RED SOX
NL: **Lance Berkman**
CARDINALS

MANAGER OF THE YEAR
AL: **Joe Maddon**
RAYS
NL: **Kirk Gibson**
DIAMONDBACKS

HANK AARON AWARD
AL: **Jose Bautista**
BLUE JAYS
NL: **Matt Kemp**
DODGERS

ROBERTO CLEMENTE AWARD
(for community service)
◀◀◀ **David Ortiz**
RED SOX

2011 Stat Leaders

AL HITTING LEADERS

HOME RUNS: **43**
Jose Bautista, BLUE JAYS

RBI: **119**
Curtis Granderson, YANKEES

AVERAGE: **.344**
Miguel Cabrera, TIGERS ▶▶▶

STOLEN BASES: **49**
Coco Crisp, ATHLETICS
Brett Gardner, YANKEES

HITS: **213**
Adrian Gonzalez, RED SOX
Michael Young, RANGERS

NL HITTING LEADERS

HOME RUNS: **39**
Matt Kemp, DODGERS

RBI: **126**
Matt Kemp, DODGERS

AVERAGE: **.337**
Jose Reyes, METS

STOLEN BASES: **61**
Michael Bourn, ASTROS/BRAVES

HITS: **207**
Starlin Castro, CUBS

AL PITCHING LEADERS

WINS: **24**
Justin Verlander, TIGERS

SAVES: **49**
Jose Valverde, TIGERS

ERA: **2.40**
Justin Verlander, TIGERS

STRIKEOUTS: **250**
Justin Verlander, TIGERS

NL PITCHING LEADERS

WINS: **21**
Clayton Kershaw, DODGERS
Ian Kennedy, DIAMONDBACKS

SAVES: **46**
John Axford, BREWERS
Craig Kimbrel, BRAVES

ERA: **2.28**
Clayton Kershaw, DODGERS

STRIKEOUTS: **248**
Clayton Kershaw, DODGERS

Around the Bases: 2012

PERFECT X 3 = WOW!

For the first time in baseball history, three perfect games were thrown in the same season.

Felix Hernandez ▶▶▶

"King Felix" tossed the first perfecto in Mariners history on August 15, beating the Rays, 1–0. He had 12 strikeouts as Seattle became the first team to throw a perfect game and have one thrown against them in the same season.

Matt Cain

With 14 strikeouts, Cain tied a perfect-game record set by the great **Sandy Koufax** on the way to a 10–0 win over the Astros on June 13. Cain became the first Giants player with a perfect game. He got help from his defense, which made two great plays on long outfield drives.

Philip Humber

In his first complete game in the Majors, Humber won only his 12th career game by beating the Mariners, 4–0, on April 21. It was the third perfecto in White Sox history; **Mark Buehrle** had the most recent before Humber in 2009.

HISTORIC HAMILTON

You think perfect games are rare? There have now been 22 of them. However, only 15 other players have done what **Josh Hamilton** did on May 8 against Baltimore. The Texas Rangers slugger hit four home runs, one of the rarest offensive feats in baseball. Each of his shots were two-run bombs, so he also had eight RBI in the game. The last player before Hamilton with four dingers in one game was **Carlos Delgado** in 2003. The first player (since 1900) to accomplish the feat? The great **Lou Gehrig** way back in 1932.

A DIFFERENT KIND OF BALL

Magic Johnson became famous for his basketball skills. Since retiring, he has become a successful businessman. In March 2012, he was part of a group that bought the Los Angeles Dodgers for a record $2.15 billion. Johnson hopes to turn around Dodgers fans' feelings about the team, which had suffered under the previous owners.

Fenway Turns 100

Ballparks are very special places to Americans. In 2012, one of the most famous ballparks ever turned 100. Fenway Park in Boston opened in 1912 and it has been filled with fans and memories ever since. The Red Sox had ceremonies all summer long marking the occasion. Trivia time: The huge wall in left field known as The Green Monster wasn't painted green until 1947 . . . the Monster seats were only added in 2003.

BASEBALL HISTORY NOTES

* On April 15, the Dodgers turned a 2-5-6-3 triple play, the first such play recorded since 1882!

* Knuckleballer **R. A. Dickey** of the Mets had a tremendous season. At one point, he threw back-to-back one-hitters, only the tenth guy to do that.

* **Aaron Hill** of the Diamondbacks hit for the cycle twice in 2012. He was only the fourth player since 1931 to get a single, double, triple, and homer in the same game two times in one year.

* Leading a historic resurgence by the Pittsburgh Pirates, outfielder **Andrew McCutcheon** had his eyes on the team's first MVP since 1992.

* With his 631st home run, **Alex Rodriguez** of the Yankees moved to fifth all-time, passing **Ken Griffey Jr.**

* On June 3, **Steve Lombardozzi** and **Bryce Harper** of the Nationals became the first rookies to lead off a game with back-to-back homers.

Hall of Fame Heroes

At an induction ceremony in August, the Baseball Hall of Fame welcomed two infielders who played in the Midwest. **Ron Santo** was a star third baseman for the Chicago Cubs in the 1960s. He never made it to the World Series, but he was beloved by Cubbies fans. He was a longtime broadcaster for the team, too. Late in his life, he battled diabetes, but he also spent a lot of time helping others with the disease. **Barry Larkin** (left) helped the Cincinnati Reds win the 1990 World Series. He was also the 1995 NL MVP and a 12-time All-Star. Larkin also won nine Silver Slugger awards as the top hitter at his position. Larkin is a regular commentator on ESPN, so fans can get the benefit of his Hall of Fame wisdom!

2012 WORLD SERIES

This year's Series had to go a long way to live up to the excitement of the 2011 Series (page 70). By the time you read this, of course, you'll know what happened. See how well we did in predicting the result!

★ TEXAS RANGERS ★
OVER
LOS ANGELES DODGERS

The New Playoffs

In 2012, Major League Baseball changed the postseason for the first time ever. What did you think of the new game? As in the past, the three division winners made the playoffs. This year, instead of one wild-card team, there were two. They played each other in a single-game playoff. The winner then joined the other three teams in the Division Series. MLB hopes that the added game gives more teams (and their fans) the chance to enjoy playoff excitement. How do you think it worked this year?

2012 Top Rookies

Baseball was blessed with an outstanding crop of great young players in 2012. These are the stars who hope to become longtime superstars, so keep an eye on them as they grow up!

BRYCE HARPER, OF, NATIONALS

He made the cover of *Sports Illustrated* when he was just 16, but he has lived up to the hype. Harper has great power and plays super defense. It's only his first year, but he already acts like a veteran. He was one of the youngest players ever to make the All-Star team, too.

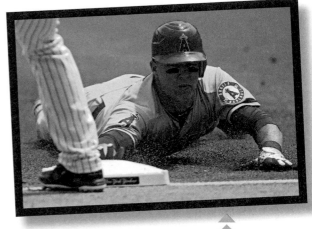

WILL MIDDLEBROOKS, 3B, RED SOX

The power and steady play of this youngster was good enough to send Boston veteran **Kevin Youkilis** packing. He could be an anchor on the infield for Boston for years.

MIKE TROUT, OF, ANGELS

No rookie has led the AL in steals and average since **Ichiro Suzuki**, but Trout was making a bid for it. The Angels phenom helped turn the team's offense around when he took over the starting job in late April.

YOENIS CESPEDES, OF, ATHLETICS

Cespedes grew up in Cuba, so he has enjoyed the freedom of both playing ball and living in America. The A's love his all-around play; he was hitting above .400 for the second half of the season.

RYAN COOK, RP, ATHLETICS

The A's thought they were sunk when closer **Andrew Bailey** was injured. Cook proved they had no such problem, taking over as the closer and earning a spot in the All-Star Game.

AN EXPENSIVE ROOKIE

The Rangers spent more than $100 million to bring Japanese pitcher **Yu Darvish** to Texas. Darvish was a superstar in Japan's pro league. In 2011, he was 19–6 with a 1.99 ERA for the Nippon Ham Fighters. (They don't fight ham; they're sponsored by a pork producer!) As one opponent said, "He's got 12 different pitches . . . and none of them are straight!"

World Series Winners

YEAR	WINNER	RUNNER-UP	SCORE*	YEAR	WINNER	RUNNER-UP	SCORE*
2011	St. Louis Cardinals	Texas Rangers	4-3	1985	Kansas City Royals	St. Louis Cardinals	4-3
2010	San Francisco Giants	Texas Rangers	4-1	1984	Detroit Tigers	San Diego Padres	4-1
2009	New York Yankees	Philadelphia Phillies	4-2	1983	Baltimore Orioles	Philadelphia Phillies	4-1
2008	Philadelphia Phillies	Tampa Bay Rays	4-1	1982	St. Louis Cardinals	Milwaukee Brewers	4-3
2007	Boston Red Sox	Colorado Rockies	4-0	1981	Los Angeles Dodgers	New York Yankees	4-2
2006	St. Louis Cardinals	Detroit Tigers	4-1	1980	Philadelphia Phillies	Kansas City Royals	4-2
2005	Chicago White Sox	Houston Astros	4-0	1979	Pittsburgh Pirates	Baltimore Orioles	4-3
2004	Boston Red Sox	St. Louis Cardinals	4-0	1978	New York Yankees	Los Angeles Dodgers	4-2
2003	Florida Marlins	New York Yankees	4-2	1977	New York Yankees	Los Angeles Dodgers	4-2
2002	Anaheim Angels	San Francisco Giants	4-3	1976	Cincinnati Reds	New York Yankees	4-0
2001	Arizona Diamondbacks	New York Yankees	4-3	1975	Cincinnati Reds	Boston Red Sox	4-3
2000	New York Yankees	New York Mets	4-1	1974	Oakland Athletics	Los Angeles Dodgers	4-1
1999	New York Yankees	Atlanta Braves	4-0	1973	Oakland Athletics	New York Mets	4-3
1998	New York Yankees	San Diego Padres	4-0	1972	Oakland Athletics	Cincinnati Reds	4-3
1997	Florida Marlins	Cleveland Indians	4-3	1971	Pittsburgh Pirates	Baltimore Orioles	4-3
1996	New York Yankees	Atlanta Braves	4-2	1970	Baltimore Orioles	Cincinnati Reds	4-1
1995	Atlanta Braves	Cleveland Indians	4-2	1969	New York Mets	Baltimore Orioles	4-1
1993	Toronto Blue Jays	Philadelphia Phillies	4-2	1968	Detroit Tigers	St. Louis Cardinals	4-3
1992	Toronto Blue Jays	Atlanta Braves	4-2	1967	St. Louis Cardinals	Boston Red Sox	4-3
1991	Minnesota Twins	Atlanta Braves	4-3	1966	Baltimore Orioles	Los Angeles Dodgers	4-0
1990	Cincinnati Reds	Oakland Athletics	4-0	1965	Los Angeles Dodgers	Minnesota Twins	4-3
1989	Oakland Athletics	San Francisco Giants	4-0	1964	St. Louis Cardinals	New York Yankees	4-3
1988	Los Angeles Dodgers	Oakland Athletics	4-1	1963	Los Angeles Dodgers	New York Yankees	4-0
1987	Minnesota Twins	St. Louis Cardinals	4-3	1962	New York Yankees	San Francisco Giants	4-3
1986	New York Mets	Boston Red Sox	4-3	1961	New York Yankees	Cincinnati Reds	4-1

* Score is represented in games played.

YEAR	WINNER	RUNNER-UP	SCORE*	YEAR	WINNER	RUNNER-UP	SCORE*
1960	Pittsburgh Pirates	New York Yankees	4-3	1931	St. Louis Cardinals	Philadelphia Athletics	4-3
1959	Los Angeles Dodgers	Chicago White Sox	4-2	1930	Philadelphia Athletics	St. Louis Cardinals	4-2
1958	New York Yankees	Milwaukee Braves	4-3	1929	Philadelphia Athletics	Chicago Cubs	4-1
1957	Milwaukee Braves	New York Yankees	4-3	1928	New York Yankees	St. Louis Cardinals	4-0
1956	New York Yankees	Brooklyn Dodgers	4-3	1927	New York Yankees	Pittsburgh Pirates	4-0
1955	Brooklyn Dodgers	New York Yankees	4-3	1926	St. Louis Cardinals	New York Yankees	4-3
1954	New York Giants	Cleveland Indians	4-0	1925	Pittsburgh Pirates	Washington Senators	4-3
1953	New York Yankees	Brooklyn Dodgers	4-2	1924	Washington Senators	New York Giants	4-3
1952	New York Yankees	Brooklyn Dodgers	4-3	1923	New York Yankees	New York Giants	4-2
1951	New York Yankees	New York Giants	4-2	1922	New York Giants	New York Yankees	4-0
1950	New York Yankees	Philadelphia Phillies	4-0	1921	New York Giants	New York Yankees	5-3
1949	New York Yankees	Brooklyn Dodgers	4-1	1920	Cleveland Indians	Brooklyn Dodgers	5-2
1948	Cleveland Indians	Boston Braves	4-2	1919	Cincinnati Reds	Chicago White Sox	5-3
1947	New York Yankees	Brooklyn Dodgers	4-3	1918	Boston Red Sox	Chicago Cubs	4-2
1946	St. Louis Cardinals	Boston Red Sox	4-3	1917	Chicago White Sox	New York Giants	4-2
1945	Detroit Tigers	Chicago Cubs	4-3	1916	Boston Red Sox	Brooklyn Dodgers	4-1
1944	St. Louis Cardinals	St. Louis Browns	4-2	1915	Boston Red Sox	Philadelphia Phillies	4-1
1943	New York Yankees	St. Louis Cardinals	4-1	1914	Boston Braves	Philadelphia Athletics	4-0
1942	St. Louis Cardinals	New York Yankees	4-1	1913	Philadelphia Athletics	New York Giants	4-1
1941	New York Yankees	Brooklyn Dodgers	4-1	1912	Boston Red Sox	New York Giants	4-3
1940	Cincinnati Reds	Detroit Tigers	4-3	1911	Philadelphia Athletics	New York Giants	4-2
1939	New York Yankees	Cincinnati Reds	4-0	1910	Philadelphia Athletics	Chicago Cubs	4-1
1938	New York Yankees	Chicago Cubs	4-0	1909	Pittsburgh Pirates	Detroit Tigers	4-3
1937	New York Yankees	New York Giants	4-1	1908	Chicago Cubs	Detroit Tigers	4-1
1936	New York Yankees	New York Giants	4-2	1907	Chicago Cubs	Detroit Tigers	4-0
1935	Detroit Tigers	Chicago Cubs	4-2	1906	Chicago White Sox	Chicago Cubs	4-2
1934	St. Louis Cardinals	Detroit Tigers	4-3	1905	New York Giants	Philadelphia Athletics	4-1
1933	New York Giants	Washington Senators	4-1	1903	Boston Red Sox	Pittsburgh Pirates	5-3
1932	New York Yankees	Chicago Cubs	4-0				

Note: 1904 not played because NL-champion Giants refused to play; 1994 not played due to MLB work stoppage.

COLLEGE BASKETBALL

A SEA OF RED
Indiana basketball fans poured out of their seats and onto the court at Assembly Hall when their men's team upset Kentucky early in the 2011–12 season. It was a great day for the Hoosiers, but Kentucky had the best day of all, wrapping up their amazing season with the NCAA championship (see page 87).

Wildcats and Bears

The two biggest stories in college basketball at the start of the 2011–12 season were the biggest stories at the end, too. The Kentucky men's team came into the season expected to be the best. The Baylor women's team earned the same prediction.

In the end, both ended up on top, something that doesn't always happen in sports. Many teams and players are expected to succeed, but seasons are long and lots of things can happen. Sometimes

FINAL MEN'S TOP 10
ESPN/USA Today

1. Kentucky
2. Kansas
3. Ohio State
4. Louisville
5. Syracuse
6. North Carolina
7. Michigan State
8. Baylor
9. Florida
10. Marquette

just meeting expectations can be harder than anything else.

Kentucky's Wildcats roared at the start of the season, losing only one of their first 33 games (see page 84). And they didn't just win . . . they ruled. Kentucky beat LSU by 24 points and South Carolina by 34. Florida was ranked No. 7 when they faced Kentucky, but the Gators lost by 20 points!

Meanwhile, Syracuse was the beast of the East. They won their first 20 games of the season before being upset by Notre Dame. Then they put together another 11-game streak that ended with a loss during the Big East Tournament. Continuing a great year for Baylor sports that began with **Robert Griffin**'s Heisman Trophy (page 61), its men's hoops teams won 17

Kentucky's Marquis Teague slams it home.

Brittney Griner was an unstoppable force.

The Wildcats were given a number-one seed in the NCAA tournament, anyway. They won six straight games in the tourney, all but two by at least 10 points. When it was all over, Kentucky had earned their eighth national title, second behind UCLA's 11.

On the women's side, **Brittney Griner** and the amazing Baylor Bears were the story from start to finish. The team had come close in recent seasons but had not cut down the nets in the end. As for Griner, few women's players have ever been as good as this 6'8" junior. She dominated every team she played. Opponents would sometimes assign three players to guard her. No problem—she just passed to her wide-open teammates. On defense? Forget it. Coaches called her the best "post" (or center) player ever.

The Bears' terrific season ended just where Griner and everyone else thought it would—at the top. Baylor defeated 12 opponents by 30 or more points, including wins of 60 and 54 points! In the NCAA tournament, Baylor was never really challenged, though Stanford gave them a good run in the semifinal.

The 2011–12 season ended just as everyone expected, with Kentucky and Baylor on top. And it sure was fun to watch it happen!

straight to start their season. In the Big 10, Ohio State ended up ranked third overall, thanks to a great NCAA tournament run and wins over three top-10-ranked teams during the season. Kentucky's only slipup came in the final game of the Southeastern Conference tournament. With the SEC's automatic bid to the NCAA on the line, Vanderbilt pulled off one of the biggest shockers of the year by beating Kentucky to win the title.

A GAME AFLOAT

The 2011–12 season started in a very unique place. North Carolina and Michigan State met on Veteran's Day . . . on an aircraft carrier! President Obama was on hand to watch the two teams play on a special court built on the deck of the U.S.S. *Carl Vinson*. North Carolina won 67–55, but the real winners were the thousands of sailors who cheered as they enjoyed two of the best teams in the nation under the evening sky.

Hoop It Up!

◀◀◀ The OTHER Team from Kentucky

College basketball fans love it when a small school plays as well as the big teams. In 2012, that team was Murray State, located in the western part of Kentucky. With only 9,000 students, it is less than a third the size of the University of Kentucky. For most of the season, however, Murray State found itself in the top 10! They didn't lose a game until February 9. Great outside shooting and tough defense were the keys to the Racers' super season.

An Ivy First

Harvard basketball was in the news in February when Jeremy Lin had his amazing streak of success (see page 98). Harvard was in the news again in March, when it earned its first trip to the NCAA tournament since 1946. The Crimson won the Ivy League outright and got that conference's automatic bid. Their Cinderella season ended early with a first-round loss to Vanderbilt, but it was a historic season for a historic school.

Game of the Year?

Two of the biggest college basketball powers in the country played one of the most dramatic games of the season. Kentucky traveled to Indiana on December 10. The Wildcats were undefeated and ranked No. 1. Indiana had not lost either. The game went back and forth. In the final two minutes, the lead changed five times.

On the final play, Indiana's Christian Watford buried a three-point shot as the buzzer sounded. Indiana won 73–72. Red-clad fans poured on to the court (page 80). It was the first win by the Hoosiers over a No. 1 team in a decade.

A Rivalry Ends?

Missouri and Kansas are neighbors on a map, and rivals on the basketball court. The two state schools have been playing each other every year for 105 seasons, but that rivalry ended in 2012. Beginning with the 2012–13 season, Missouri will move to the Southeastern Conference. The teams' final matchup was a memorable one. A furious comeback by Kansas tied the score. Fans in Kansas's Allen Fieldhouse rattled the roof to help their team. The noise reached 127 decibels—a jet engine puts out about 120–130 decibels—before Kansas clinched a thrilling 87–86 overtime win.

A Rivalry Continues ▶▶▶

Another famous rivalry—Duke and North Carolina—will continue, but it will have to go a long way to top the thrilling finish of its February 8 game. UNC controlled the game for most of the way, leading by 10 with less than three minutes to play. However, in front of a stunned Tar Heels crowd, Duke roared back. As the clock ticked down, Duke freshman guard **Austin Rivers** shot a game-winning three-point buzzer-beater.

Wide Wingspan

Kentucky's **Anthony Davis** has a wide wingspan. He is 6′10″, but his arms can reach as wide as 7′4″! Those arms and great skill have made him a record-setting shot blocker. His 186 blocks in 2011–12 set a new freshman record at Kentucky. That was more than some entire teams!

PLAYERS OF THE YEAR

◀ **MEN: Anthony Davis** The Kentucky star was only the second freshman ever to win the AP Player of the Year Award. He also won the Wooden Award and the Naismith Award, despite having the lowest points-per-game average of any award winner. Instead, it was his defensive powers that helped him dominate.

WOMEN: Brittney Griner ▶ This was easy for voters. Griner was clearly the best player in the country, and she won every major award offered: AP Player of the Year, Wade Trophy, and the Naismith Award. Bad news for opponents: She's back at Baylor for one more season.

March Madness I!

MEN'S 2012 NCAA TOURNAMENT

Norfolk had a huge upset in the first round.

First and Second Rounds

▶ Before March 16, only four No. 15 seeds had ever won their opening games against No. 2 seeds. Then on that wild Friday, it happened twice! First, Norfolk State beat mighty Missouri, 86–84. Then surprising Lehigh beat Duke, 75–70. The first round is all about upsets!

▶ Another upset came in the Midwest Regional. No. 13 Ohio defeated No. 4 Michigan, 65–60. Ohio continued its run in the second round, beating fellow longshot South Florida (a No. 12 seed) to become the first 13 seed to make the Sweet Sixteen since 2006.

▶ North Carolina State, at No. 11, also made the Sweet Sixteen after upsetting San Diego State and Georgetown.

Sweet Sixteen

▶ Four teams from Ohio—Ohio State, Cincinnati, Ohio, and Xavier—made the Sweet Sixteen, the first time any state sent that many.

▶ No teams west of Texas made it to this round for the first time.

▶ No. 13 Ohio almost made history, taking No. 1 UNC into overtime before falling, 73–66.

▶ No. 1 Syracuse won by only one point over Wisconsin, 64–63.

▶ Louisville's late-season success continued as they knocked off No. 1 Michigan State, 57–44.

▶ Kentucky became the first team in the 2012 tournament to reach 100 points in a game. They needed all of them, beating Indiana 102–90 to avenge an early-season loss (see page 80).

Elite Eight

▶ Louisville earned a trip to the Final Four by beating No. 7 Florida. Their win made it four years in a row with a team from the Big East in the last round.

▶ Kentucky held off a tough Baylor team. The Wildcats had a 23-point lead in the first half, but the Bears narrowed that in the second before Kentucky pulled away for the win.

▶ Kansas ended their victory over North Carolina on a 12–0 run.

▶ Powerful Syracuse saw its dream season end early as Ohio State beat them 77–70.

Ohio State beat former No. 1 Syracuse.

half, the Kansas defense stepped up. The Jayhawks held OSU to 29 percent shooting while ramping up their own offense. With just over 90 seconds left, Kansas grabbed the lead for good and held on for the win.

Championship Game

Old Kentucky's Home

For the eighth time, the second-most ever, Kentucky cut down the nets as the NCAA champion. Their victory against Kansas was never really in doubt. The Wildcats were ahead early, at one point stomping the Jayhawks by 25 points. Kansas fought back in the second half, cutting the lead to only five, but Kentucky held on. The Wildcats started three freshmen and two sophomores, one of the youngest teams ever to win it all. The final score was 67–59.

Final Four

SEMIFINAL: Battle of the Bluegrass State

Both teams in the first semifinal hailed from Kentucky. The University of Kentucky came into the tournament ranked number one. Louisville was riding an eight-game winning streak entering this game, after winning the Big East. Kentucky got out early, but Louisville roared back to tie the game, 49–49. Kentucky then pulled away again and held off a determined Cardinals team. The win sent Kentucky to their 11th NCAA championship game.

SEMIFINAL: Big Twos

A pair of No. 2 seeds battled in the other semifinal. For most of the game, it looked like Ohio State would join Kentucky in the final. However, in the second

Winning players each cut a loop of the net for a souvenir.

March Madness II!

WOMEN'S 2012 NCAA TOURNAMENT

UConn and Notre Dame went to OT in a semi.

First and Second Rounds

▶ Delaware's high-scoring **Elena Delle Donne** scored 39 points in her team's win over Arkansas–Little Rock.

▶ Baylor didn't just beat UC Santa Barbara—they demolished them, 81–40.

▶ The biggest upset of the first round was No. 13 Marist over No. 4 Georgia.

▶ In a second-round win, Connecticut held Kansas State to a tournament-low 26 points.

Sweet Sixteen

▶ Defending champ Texas A&M lost to Maryland, ending their repeat chance.

▶ No. 11 Kansas made it as far as the Sweet Sixteen, but their upset streak ended with a loss to No. 2 Tennessee.

▶ On its way to the championship game, Notre Dame's defense was the star, allowing fewer than 50 points in three of their four wins.

Final Four

SEMIFINAL: 0 for 4

Stanford had won 32 straight games and had made the Final Four for the fourth straight year . . . but once again, they also lost there for the fourth straight year. Senior star **Nnemkadi Ogwumike** wrapped up her sterling career frustrated after the Cardinal lost to mighty Baylor 59–47. Ogwumike had 22 points, but that was not enough to overcome Griner and the Bears.

SEMIFINAL: Overtime Thriller

UConn trailed late in the game, but thanks to clutch free throws by **Kelly Faris**, tied the game at 67–67 as the final buzzer sounded. That sent their game against Notre Dame into overtime. It was the second year in a row the two hoops powerhouses met in the semis, but the result was the same. Notre Dame's **Brittany**

Delle Donne averaged 28.1 points per game.

FINAL WOMEN'S TOP 10
ESPN/USA Today

1. Baylor
2. Notre Dame
3. Stanford
4. Connecticut
5. Maryland
6. Duke
7. Tennessee
8. Kentucky
9. Penn State
10. Georgia Tech

Griner led Baylor to the net-cutting moment.

Mallory hit two big three-point shots and the Irish outscored the Huskies 16–8 in the overtime period to win the game.

Championship Game

Just as in the men's final, this game didn't hold much excitement. Baylor shot an amazing 63 percent and led by as many as 25 points. They became the first team,

men's or women's, to finish a season 40–0. **Brittney Griner** was named the Final Four Most Outstanding Player after scoring 26 points in the final. At one point, she was guarded by three Notre Dame players. But she spun once, lifted the ball way over her opponents' heads, and banked in a soft jumper. Baylor coach **Kim Mulkey** became the first person ever to win an NCAA title as a player, an assistant coach, and a head coach. Notre Dame lost, 80–61, its second straight defeat in the final game.

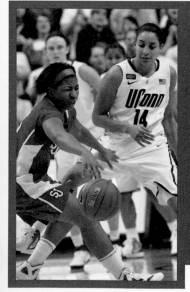

2011–12 Season Highlights

◄◄◄**STREAKS STRUCK** Through January 2012, Duke's women had won 34 straight home games. That streak ended with a loss to mighty Connecticut, the 2010 NCAA champions. UConn had its own streak broken a month later. St. John's became the first visiting team to beat the Huskies since 2007, a run of 99 straight games.

UPSET OUT WEST BYU's power scoring had led it to a No. 23 ranking when it welcomed the University of San Francisco. USF had won only two games in their conference, so BYU figured on an easy win. But the Cougars started out cold and got colder, making only two of their 20 three-point attempts. USF won 71–64 in one of the biggest upsets of the year.

NCAA Champs!

MEN'S DIVISION I

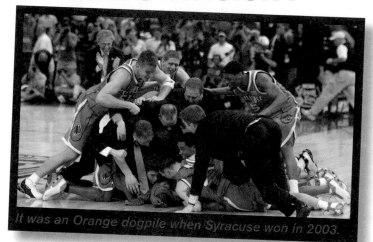

It was an Orange dogpile when Syracuse won in 2003.

2012 **Kentucky**	2001 **Duke**	1990 **UNLV**
2011 **Connecticut**	2000 **Michigan State**	1989 **Michigan**
2010 **Duke**	1999 **Connecticut**	1988 **Kansas**
2009 **North Carolina**	1998 **Kentucky**	1987 **Indiana**
2008 **Kansas**	1997 **Arizona**	1986 **Louisville**
2007 **Florida**	1996 **Kentucky**	1985 **Villanova**
2006 **Florida**	1995 **UCLA**	1984 **Georgetown**
2005 **North Carolina**	1994 **Arkansas**	1983 **NC State**
2004 **Connecticut**	1993 **North Carolina**	1982 **North Carolina**
2003 **Syracuse**	1992 **Duke**	1981 **Indiana**
2002 **Maryland**	1991 **Duke**	1980 **Louisville**
		1979 **Michigan State**
		1978 **Kentucky**
		1977 **Marquette**
		1976 **Indiana**
		1975 **UCLA**
		1974 **NC State**
		1973 **UCLA**
		1972 **UCLA**
		1971 **UCLA**

1970 **UCLA**	1947 **Holy Cross**	1942 **Stanford**
1969 **UCLA**	1946 **Oklahoma A&M**	1941 **Wisconsin**
1968 **UCLA**	1945 **Oklahoma A&M**	1940 **Indiana**
1967 **UCLA**	1944 **Utah**	1939 **Oregon**
1966 **Texas Western**	1943 **Wyoming**	
1965 **UCLA**		
1964 **UCLA**		

WOMEN'S DIVISION I

1963 **Loyola (Illinois)**	2012 **Baylor**	1996 **Tennessee**
1962 **Cincinnati**	2011 **Texas A&M**	1995 **Connecticut**
1961 **Cincinnati**	2010 **Connecticut**	1994 **North Carolina**
1960 **Ohio State**	2009 **Connecticut**	1993 **Texas Tech**
1959 **California**	2008 **Tennessee**	1992 **Stanford**
1958 **Kentucky**	2007 **Tennessee**	1991 **Tennessee**
1957 **North Carolina**	2006 **Maryland**	1990 **Stanford**
1956 **San Francisco**	2005 **Baylor**	1989 **Tennessee**
1955 **San Francisco**	2004 **Connecticut**	1988 **Louisiana Tech**
1954 **La Salle**	2003 **Connecticut**	1987 **Tennessee**
1953 **Indiana**	2002 **Connecticut**	1986 **Texas**
1952 **Kansas**	2001 **Notre Dame**	1985 **Old Dominion**
1951 **Kentucky**	2000 **Connecticut**	1984 **USC**
1950 **City Coll. of N.Y.**	1999 **Purdue**	1983 **USC**
1949 **Kentucky**	1998 **Tennessee**	1982 **Louisiana Tech**
1948 **Kentucky**	1997 **Tennessee**	

THE KING AND THE PRINCE

The NBA Finals matched a reigning superstar, LeBron James (left), against a rising young team, the Oklahoma City Thunder. To find out who came out on top, check out page 97.

NBA

NBA 2012

Miami's "Big 3" finally got to celebrate.

The theme for the 2011–12 NBA season was The Big Three: Take Two. After **LeBron James** made "the Decision" to move to Miami in 2010, the Heat were expected to win it all. Dallas got in the way, though, so in 2011–12, James and his Heat teammates wanted revenge.

They had to wait a while, however. The 2011–12 NBA season started late. After the NBA owners and players could not agree on a new contract, the NBA "locked out" the players. That is, they didn't let them practice or play games. Until mid-December, some experts were worried that the entire season might be canceled.

However, at the last minute, to NBA fans' relief, a deal was made. The NBA started its season on December 25, almost two months late. The league created a new schedule, with each team playing 66 games. A normal season includes 82 games.

Once the balls started bouncing, a couple of "new" teams jumped into the national picture. They were not new teams, just new to the tops of their divisions.

In the West, the Los Angeles Clippers stunned many experts by spending much of the season ahead of the Lakers. A lot of their success was due to new point guard **Chris Paul**, one of the most talented all-around players in the league. Of course, having mega-dunkster **Blake Griffin** to pass to really helped.

In the Midwest, it was something old and something new. Something old was the San Antonio Spurs, owners of four NBA titles with an eye on a fifth. **Tim Duncan** just never seems to get old. With his supporting cast of **Tony Parker** and **Manu Ginobili** firing in

Paul was L.A.'s new hoops star.

Durant scored an NBA-best 28 points per game.

outside shots, the Spurs are always solid. However, this season the young Oklahoma City Thunder rose to the top. Led by three-time scoring champ **Kevin Durant** and guard **Russell Westbrook**, the Thunder excited their loyal fans by romping through the season. The Chicago Bulls had the best regular-season record, winning 50 games. They depended heavily on returning league MVP **Derrick Rose**, however. When Rose went down early in the playoffs with a knee injury, it was lights out in Chicago.

In the East, two teams rose above the others (though a third team, the Knicks, had one of the biggest stories of the season—see page 98). Miami had its amazing 1-2-3 punch of James (who won his third MVP award), **Dwyane Wade**, and **Chris Bosh**, but they still struggled at times. By the end of the season, though, they were jelling beautifully. Meanwhile, the aging Celtics gave it one more run. Their own trio of **Paul Pierce**, **Kevin Garnett**, and **Ray Allen** are getting older, and this might have been their last shot as a group. (In fact, after the season, Allen signed with the Heat.)

Even though the season started late, the action was fierce and fans quickly got back on board. In the end, after a fierce NBA Finals fight, the Heat were the hottest. For LeBron James, it was "Mission: Accomplished."

2011–12 FINAL STANDINGS

EASTERN CONFERENCE

ATLANTIC DIVISION	W–L
Celtics	39–27
Knicks	36–30
76ers	35–31
Raptors	23–43
Nets	22–44

CENTRAL DIVISION	W–L
Bulls	50–16
Pacers	42–24
Bucks	31–35
Pistons	25–41
Cavaliers	21–45

SOUTHEAST DIVISION	W–L
Heat	46–20
Hawks	40–26
Magic	37–29
Wizards	20–46
Bobcats	7–59

WESTERN CONFERENCE

NORTHWEST DIVISION	W–L
Thunder	47–19
Nuggets	38–28
Jazz	36–30
Trail Blazers	28–38
Timberwolves	26–40

SOUTHWEST DIVISION	W–L
Spurs	50–16
Grizzlies	41–25
Mavericks	36–30
Rockets	34–42
Hornets	21–45

PACIFIC DIVISION	W–L
Lakers	41–25
Clippers	40–26
Suns	33–33
Warriors	23–43
Kings	22–44

NBA Playoffs

FIRST ROUND HIGHLIGHTS

➤ Chicago had the East's best record. Their playoff hopes were dashed when star guard **Chris Rose** injured his knee.

➤ The Lakers' **Andrew Bynum** had the team's first triple-double in 21 years leading L.A. over the Denver Nuggets.

➤ The surprising Clippers trailed by 27 points in Game 1, but came back to beat the Memphis Grizzlies.

SEMIFINALS

➤ The San Antonio Spurs ended the Clippers' magic season in four games.

➤ The Oklahoma City Thunder sent the powerful Lakers home in a thrilling five-game series.

➤ The Indiana Pacers made it exciting, but the Miami Heat took another step toward returning to the NBA Finals.

Bynum had a huge game against Denver.

Griffin led a mighty Clippers comeback.

CONFERENCE FINALS

➤ The Spurs charged to wins in the first two games over the Thunder. It didn't look good for **Kevin Durant** and Co. However, the young guns of Oklahoma City reeled off four straight wins to capture their first Western Conference championship.

➤ In one of the most exciting series in the playoffs, it took all seven games to sort out a champion. It was between the Heat and the Celtics. In the end, led by MVP **LeBron James**, the Heat finally closed out the Celtics to win the conference title for the second year in a row.

NBA Finals

GAME 1
Thunder 105, Heat 94

Down by 18 points in the first half, Oklahoma City rode the wide shoulders of **Kevin Durant** to an amazing comeback. Durant had 17 of his 36 points in the fourth quarter. The Thunder's fans were thunderously loud as they helped rally their team to a big win at home.

GAME 2
Heat 100, Thunder 96

LeBron James was not going to let Durant steal his . . . thunder. The MVP led the Heat to an 18–2 start and ended up scoring 32 points. The Thunder nearly pulled off another big comeback, but fell just short at the end.

GAME 3
Heat 91, Thunder 85

Foul trouble kept Durant from performing at his best, but nothing stopped

In his ninth NBA season, James was finally a champ.

James, who scored 29 points in leading the Heat to their second straight victory.

GAME 4
Heat 104, Thunder 98

Guts. That's what James needed in this game . . . good old-fashioned guts. Leg cramps hobbled the star in the second half, but he battled through them. His gutsy three-point shot tied the game late and the Heat held on for their third win, even as OKC's **Russell Westbrook** scored a playoff-high 43 points.

GAME 5
Heat 121, Thunder 106

The outcome was never really in doubt as the Heat rolled to their second NBA championship with a convincing win. Miami got out to a lead as big as Mike Miller made seven three-point shots. At the end, the confetti flew as the hometown fans cheered their Big Three. Miami: NBA champs.

Hoop Notes

LINSANITY!

The biggest story of the NBA season was not the lockout or who won the NBA title. It was a backup point guard from Harvard.

Jeremy Lin was a star player at that famous university, but he was the first player from Harvard to make the NBA in more than 50 years. He played briefly for Golden State, but they cut him just before the 2011–12 season. The Knicks signed him after two of their guards were hurt. He was still a backup, though, and ended up in the Knicks' minor leagues.

In February, he got his shot. And that's when the magic started. In his first seven games, Lin scored more points than **Michael Jordan**, **Wilt Chamberlain**, and **Kobe Bryant** scored in their first seven games. He led the Knicks to a seven-game winning streak that put them on the road to the playoffs. His amazing passing and deadly shooting, plus his unlikely story, made him front-page news around the world. He was also the first player of Taiwanese descent to make the NBA.

Unfortunately, a knee injury kept Lin from helping the Knicks in the playoffs. Still, his amazing rise from "nowhere" delighted fans everywhere.

A SEASON TO FORGET

The Charlotte Bobcats had the worst season of any team in NBA history. Here are some of the lowlights:

➤ Worst winning percentage ever: 10.6 (their record was 7–59)
➤ They had a 23-game losing streak
➤ They lost 24 games by 20 points or more.
➤ They lost 9 games by 30 points or more.

NBA NOTES

➤ In a game in January 2012, the Bucks and Pistons set a record by making all 41 of their combined free-throw attempts.

➤ Speaking of free throws in January, **Dwight Howard** had a record 39 attempts in one game; he made 21 of them.

◀◀◀ The Nets' **Deron Williams** had the season's biggest scoring binge, with 57 in a game in March. It was also a Nets team record.

➤ One of the highest-scoring games in recent seasons was a 149–140 double-OT win by the Thunder over the Timberwolves.

Points Galore

In a season that celebrated the 50th anniversary of **Wilt Chamberlain** scoring an NBA-record 100 points in a game in 1962, players outside the NBA made the scoring news.

In the American Basketball Association, the Jacksonville Giants poured in a stunning 211 points in a game in February, easily beating the Columbus Riverballers. The most before then was 186 points, scored in a 1983 game by the Pistons and in a 1991 college game by Loyola Marymount. In a 48-minute game, the Giants scored more than four points every minute!

Also, props to **Mohammad El Akkari**, who scored 113 points all by himself in a pro league in Lebanon.

NBA Awards

MVP: LeBron James, HEAT
"King James" won his third league MVP award as he led Miami to the NBA title. Scoring champ Kevin Durant and Clippers hero Chris Paul finished second and third in the voting.

DEFENSIVE PLAYER OF THE YEAR:
   Tyson Chandler, KNICKS

ROOKIE OF THE YEAR:
   Kyrie Irving, CAVALIERS

SIXTH MAN OF THE YEAR:
   James Harden, THUNDER

2011 WNBA

Augustus was the key link for the Lynx.

The Lynx made it clear early in the 2011 WNBA season that they intended to win their first league title. They missed the playoffs for six years through 2009. They had struggled so much that they often had top draft picks. But all the struggle finally paid off and the Lynx dominated the 2011 season.

Minnesota made a strong statement early, winning 13 of its first 14 games. The Lynx didn't depend on one star, however. Six different players on their team led them in scoring in at least one game. **Seimone Augustus**, a former rookie of the year, was a key leader, however. The 2011 rookie of the year, former Connecticut star **Maya Moore**, proved she was ready for the pros, too.

In the East, the Atlanta Dream had a tougher road. In only their fourth season, the Dream was led by **Angel McCoughtry**. Coming off a WNBA Finals loss, they had high hopes, but then lost 9 of their first 12 games. But starting in mid-July, they went 17–5 to finish strong. They beat the Indiana Fever to earn their second straight Eastern Conference title and met Minnesota in the WNBA Finals.

WNBA 2011 Stats Leaders

✳ **SCORING:** Diana Taurasi, Phoenix, 21.6 points per game
✳ **REBOUNDING:** Tina Charles, Conn., 11.0 rebounds per game
✳ **ASSISTS:** Lindsay Whalen, Minnesota, 5.9 assists per game.

2011 WNBA MVP

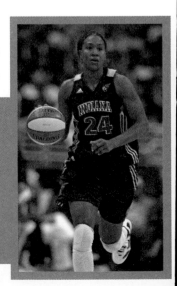

Tamika Catchings of the Indiana Fever had come oh-so-close to winning the MVP award during her 10-year career. She was among the top three in the voting five times, including finishing second three times. In 2011, she finally finished on top, earning her first WNBA MVP award. The power forward led the Fever to the East's best record while averaging 15.5 points and 7.1 rebounds per game.

2011 WNBA FINALS

GAME 1
Lynx 88, Dream 74

With Game 1 tied at the start of the fourth quarter, it looked like defense would win the day. The Lynx blocked a WNBA Finals record 11 shots and held the Dream to 37 percent shooting. Minnesota won the fourth quarter, 26–12, and the all-important opening game.

GAME 2
Lynx 101, Dream 95

Minnesota's **Seimone Augustus** would have set a new WNBA Finals scoring record with 36 points, leading her Lynx team to its second victory. She *would* have set it except that Dream guard **Angel McCoughtry** scored 38 points in the same game! Together they set a record for most points by a pair of opponents.

Lindsay Whalen helped Minnesota win.

2011 WNBA FINAL STANDINGS
REGULAR SEASON

EASTERN CONFERENCE		WESTERN CONFERENCE	
Indiana Fever	21–13	Minnesota Lynx	27–7
Connecticut Sun	21–13	Seattle Storm	21–13
Atlanta Dream	20–14	Phoenix Mercury	19–15
New York Liberty	19–15	San Antonio Silver Stars	18–16
Chicago Sky	14–20	Los Angeles Sparks	15–19
Washington Mystics	6–28	Tulsa Shock	3–31

GAME 3
Lynx 73, Dream 67

Tough defense was the key again, as Augustus held her opposite number McCoughtry to "only" 22 points. The other Dream players couldn't pick up the slack. Led by star **Maya Moore** and Augustus, the Lynx won their first WNBA title with the three-game sweep.

Stat Stuff

NBA CHAMPIONS

2011–12 **Miami**	2008–09 **L.A. Lakers**	1993–94 **Houston**
2010–11 **Dallas**	2007–08 **Boston**	1992–93 **Chicago**
2009–10 **L.A. Lakers**	2006–07 **San Antonio**	1991–92 **Chicago**
	2005–06 **Miami**	1990–91 **Chicago**
	2004–05 **San Antonio**	1989–90 **Detroit**
	2003–04 **Detroit**	1988–89 **Detroit**
	2002–03 **San Antonio**	1987–88 **L.A. Lakers**
	2001–02 **L.A. Lakers**	1986–87 **L.A. Lakers**
	2000–01 **L.A. Lakers**	1985–86 **Boston**
	1999–00 **L.A. Lakers**	1984–85 **L.A. Lakers**
	1998–99 **San Antonio**	1983–84 **Boston**
	1997–98 **Chicago**	1982–83 **Philadelphia**
	1996–97 **Chicago**	1981–82 **L.A. Lakers**
	1995–96 **Chicago**	1980–81 **Boston**
	1994–95 **Houston**	1979–80 **L.A. Lakers**

Dr. J, Julius Erving, led Philly in 1983.

1978-79 **Seattle**	1960-61 **Boston**	1952-53 **Minneapolis**
1977-78 **Washington**	1959-60 **Boston**	1951-52 **Minneapolis**
1976-77 **Portland**	1958-59 **Boston**	1950-51 **Rochester**
1975-76 **Boston**	1957-58 **St. Louis**	1949-50 **Minneapolis**
1974-75 **Golden State**	1956-57 **Boston**	1948-49 **Minneapolis**
1973-74 **Boston**	1955-56 **Philadelphia**	1947-48 **Baltimore**
1972-73 **New York**	1954-55 **Syracuse**	1946-47 **Philadelphia**
1971-72 **L.A. Lakers**	1953-54 **Minneapolis**	
1970-71 **Milwaukee**		
1969-70 **New York**		
1968-69 **Boston**		
1967-68 **Boston**		
1966-67 **Philadelphia**		
1965-66 **Boston**		
1964-65 **Boston**		
1963-64 **Boston**		
1962-63 **Boston**		
1961-62 **Boston**		

WNBA CHAMPIONS

2011 **Minnesota**	2003 **Detroit**
2010 **Seattle**	2002 **Los Angeles**
2009 **Phoenix**	2001 **Los Angeles**
2008 **Detroit**	2000 **Houston**
2007 **Phoenix**	1999 **Houston**
2006 **Detroit**	1998 **Houston**
2005 **Sacramento**	1997 **Houston**
2004 **Seattle**	

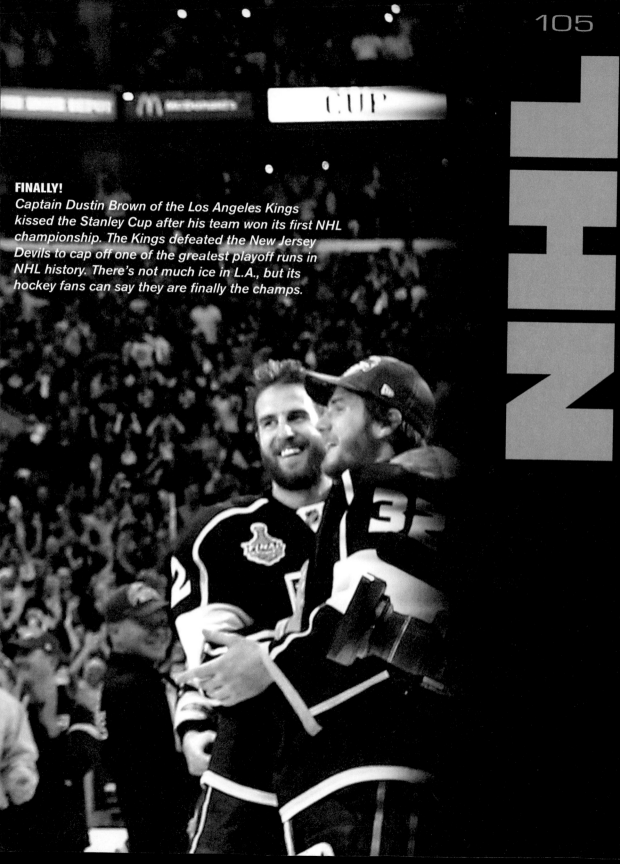

CUP

NHL

FINALLY!
*Captain Dustin Brown of the Los Angeles Kings
kissed the Stanley Cup after his team won its first NHL
championship. The Kings defeated the New Jersey
Devils to cap off one of the greatest playoff runs in
NHL history. There's not much ice in L.A., but its
hockey fans can say they are finally the champs.*

2011-12 Season

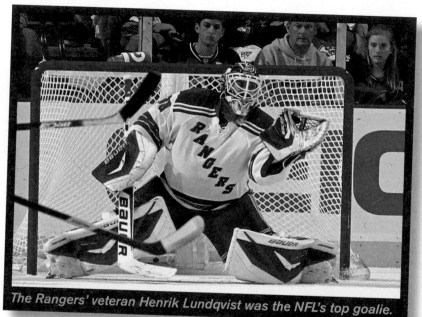

The Rangers' veteran Henrik Lundqvist was the NFL's top goalie.

challenged for the number-one spot in the Eastern Conference for most of the season.

The New York Rangers, however, were the team the Bruins and others chased for the Eastern Conference crown most of the season. The Rangers were led by the Vezina Trophy–winning goaltender **Henrik Lundqvist**. He became the first goalie in NHL history with 30 or more wins in each of his first seven seasons. New York also relied on winger **Marian Gaborik** and his 41 goals, as well as several talented young defensemen. The Rangers improved by 16 points and finished first in the East.

The new kings of hockey are . . . the Kings! For the first time in their 45-year history, the Los Angeles Kings won the Stanley Cup, thrilling their loyal fans. After finishing only third in their division and earning the final playoff spot, the Kings roared through the postseason to win the Cup.

Early in the season, the defending-champion Boston Bruins were a favorite to repeat as champs. With **Tim Thomas** in goal, giant defenseman **Zdeno Chara** blasting shots from the point and some hard-working forwards, the Bruins

In the West, the dynamic duo of **Henrik** and **Daniel Sedin** again led the Vancouver Canucks to the top of the Western Conference. After their defeat in the 2011 Stanley Cup Final, the Canucks played the 2011–12 season with fiery determination. They were chased by another of the league's most improved teams, the St. Louis Blues. The Blues were almost impossible to score on thanks to their super goaltending duo of

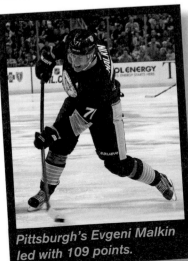

Pittsburgh's Evgeni Malkin led with 109 points.

Jets rejoiced as hockey returned to Winnipeg.

Jaroslav Halak and **Brian Elliott**. The Blues finished the season an amazing 23 points better than the previous season.

Fans watched anxiously for the return of concussion victim **Sidney Crosby**, but the Penguins winger didn't return until November. He played 12 games before returning to the sidelines again. Crosby's absence gave other great NHL players an opportunity to get their share of the spotlight. Crosby's teammate **Evgeni Malkin** carried the load for the Penguins and led the league in scoring. But it was the superstar scoring of **Steven Stamkos**, playing for the struggling Tampa Bay Lightning, and the nifty skills of sniper **Claude Giroux** of the Philadelphia Flyers that had fans' pulses racing.

Winnipeg hockey fans had one of the happiest days of their lives when the puck was dropped at the start of an October 9 game against the Montreal Canadiens. It marked the return of the Winnipeg Jets to the NHL. The hometown fans showed their love for their team by filling the MTS Centre to capacity for every Jets home game.

In the end, though, it was the fans of Los Angeles who finally got to watch a Stanley Cup parade in their sunny hometown.

FINAL STANDINGS

EASTERN CONFERENCE	PTS
New York **Rangers**	109
Pittsburgh **Penguins**	108
Philadelphia **Flyers**	103
Boston **Bruins**	102
New Jersey **Devils**	102
Florida **Panthers**	94
Washington **Capitals**	92
Ottawa **Senators**	92
Buffalo **Sabres**	89
Tampa Bay **Lightning**	84
Winnipeg **Jets**	84
Carolina **Hurricanes**	82
Toronto **Maple Leafs**	80
New York **Islanders**	79
Montreal **Canadiens**	78

WESTERN CONFERENCE	PTS
Vancouver **Canucks**	111
St. Louis **Blues**	109
Nashville **Predators**	104
Detroit **Red Wings**	102
Chicago **Blackhawks**	101
Phoenix **Coyotes**	97
San Jose **Sharks**	96
Los Angeles **Kings**	95
Calgary **Flames**	90
Dallas **Stars**	89
Colorado **Avalanche**	88
Minnesota **Wild**	81
Anaheim **Ducks**	80
Edmonton **Oilers**	74
Columbus **Blue Jackets**	65

Stanley Cup Playoffs

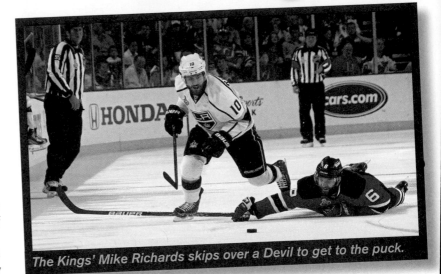

The Kings' Mike Richards skips over a Devil to get to the puck.

At the end of game five of the Stanley Cup Finals, Los Angeles Kings captain **Dustin Brown** said, "I don't know what 45 years of pent-up energy sounds like, but if we play our game, maybe we'll find out." One game later, he did. Wrapping up one of the most improbable playoff runs in recent NHL history, the Los Angeles Kings blew out the New Jersey Devils 6–1 in Game 6 to win their first Stanley Cup.

The 2012 Stanley Cup playoffs were filled with surprises. First, the defending-champion Bruins lost to the Washington Capitals in seven games. Then the Kings beat the top-seeded Vancouver Canucks. L.A. goalie **Jonathan Quick** gave up only eight goals in five games. Then the Penguins, late-season stars, lost in an upset to the Philadelphia Flyers.

The Kings used their win over the Canucks as a springboard. In the Western Conference semifinals, they swept the St. Louis Blues. Quick was even better, giving up only six goals in four games. In the conference final, L.A. made it three upsets in a row. They beat the No. 3 Phoenix Coyotes to earn their first trip to the Stanley Cup Final since 1993.

In the East, the New Jersey Devils' 40-year-old goaltender, **Martin Brodeur**, started the 2012 playoffs by winning his 100th career playoff game against the surprising Florida Panthers. Then his team beat the Panthers in a thrilling, double-overtime Game 7. The Devils knocked out the Flyers in five games and then their New York rival Rangers in six games to earn their trip to the Stanley Cup Finals.

The Kings were only the second eighth-seed team to make it to the Stanley Cup Finals (the 2006 Edmonton Oilers were the other), but they didn't play that way.

Brodeur was outstanding for New Jersey.

The Finals opened in New Jersey with L.A. winning 2–1 in overtime. The Kings' **Anze Kopitar** fired the puck past Brodeur for the win. Game 2 was more of the same—close checking, great goaltending, and an overtime win by the Kings, thanks to Jeff Carter's goal. In Game 3, Quick's goaltending heroics and four goals by the Kings gave them a commanding 3–0 lead in games.

The Devils won Game 4 on a wrist shot by rookie **Adam Henrique**. The Devils then dealt the Kings their first road loss of the playoffs with a 2–1 Game 5 victory on a fluke goal by defenseman **Bryce Salvador** that deflected off a Kings player. The Devils began to believe they could come all the way back.

But they didn't. In the first quarter of Game 6, the Devils committed a five-minute major penalty. Playing a man down, they gave up three goals in five minutes to the Kings. The Kings kept up the pressure and put three more pucks into the net to clinch their first Stanley Cup. All that energy Brown was worried about burst into cheers for Kings fans finally celebrating the champs.

The Penguins and Flyers set a record with 45 goals in the first four games of their series.

PLAY-OFF RESULTS
(Games won in parentheses)

FIRST ROUND

EASTERN CONFERENCE
New York OVER Ottawa (4-3)
Washington OVER Boston (4-3)
New Jersey OVER Florida (4-3)
Philadelphia OVER Pittsburgh (4-2)

WESTERN CONFERENCE
Los Angeles OVER Vancouver (4-1)
St. Louis OVER San Jose (4-1)
Phoenix OVER Chicago (4-2)
Nashville OVER Detroit (4-1)

CONFERENCE SEMIFINALS

EASTERN CONFERENCE
New York OVER Washington (4-3)
New Jersey OVER Philadelphia (4-1)

WESTERN CONFERENCE
Phoenix OVER Nashville (4-1)
Los Angeles OVER St. Louis (4-0)

CONFERENCE FINALS

EASTERN CONFERENCE
New Jersey OVER New York (4-2)

WESTERN CONFERENCE
Los Angeles OVER Phoenix (4-1)

STANLEY CUP FINALS
Los Angeles OVER New Jersey (4-2)

Hockey Highlights

Stamkos Hits 60 ▶▶▶

Steven Stamkos had a season to remember for the Tampa Bay Lightning, becoming only the second player in the last 15 years to score 60 goals in a season. He achieved the milestone in the last game. Stamkos grew as a player during 2011–12, stepping out of **Martin St. Louis**'s shadow, leading the league in goals, and finishing second in Hart Trophy balloting.

Winter Classic

The NHL held its extremely popular Winter Classic, the annual outdoor hockey game, on January 2, 2012. This year, it was a showdown at Citizens Bank Park, featuring the hometown Philadelphia Flyers and the visiting New York Rangers. The Rangers won on a pair of goals from team tough guy **Mike Rupp** and a game-winner by **Brad Richards**.

◀◀◀ All-Star Weekend

The 2012 NHL All-Star Game was held in Ottawa. The two teams were selected in a fantasy draft by captains **Daniel Alfredsson** and **Zdeno Chara**. The game had lots of scoring, with Team Chara winning the match 12–9. **Marian Gaborik** of Team Chara (and the New York Rangers) had a hat trick and was named the game's MVP. This year's big winners in the All-Star Weekend skills competition put on a great show. The Boston Bruins' Zdeno Chara won the hardest-shot competition with a record-setting 108.8 mph slapshot. New York Rangers rookie **Carl Hagelin** was the fastest skater and **Jamie Benn** of the Dallas Stars was the most accurate shooter. The biggest highlight, though, might have been Chicago Blackhawk **Patrick Kane**, putting on Clark Kent glasses and a Superman cape, stickhandling in the breakaway challenge.

In Good Company
Wayne Gretzky. Paul Coffey. Sam Gagner? Gagner added his name to Edmonton Oilers and NHL record books when

he scored eight points on four goals and four assists in a single game against the Chicago Blackhawks on February 2, 2012. The 22-year-old became the first player since 1988 to do so. He scored a pair of goals and an assist in his next game, setting an Edmonton Oilers record with 11 consecutive points.

Devilish Draft Pick
The Devils turned heads with their first pick in the 2012 Draft. In 1994, **Stephane Matteau** of the Rangers beat the Devils with an overtime goal that sent Matteau's Rangers to the Stanley Cup Finals . . . and sent the Devils home. In 2012, New Jersey got its revenge, making Matteau's son **Stefan** their first pick. Now Stephane has to root for the Devils!

◄◄◄ Farewell, Lidstrom
On May 31, 2012, the NHL and the Detroit Red Wings said good-bye to one of the greatest players in NHL history, as **Nicklas Lidstrom** announced his retirement. Lidstrom is one of the greatest defensemen of all time. He racked up an astounding seven Norris Trophies as the league's best defenseman. He was named the Red Wings' captain in 2006 and made history as the first European captain to raise the Stanley Cup, when the Red Wings won in 2008.

2011–12 Awards

Conn Smythe Trophy
(Stanley Cup Play-offs MVP)
JONATHAN QUICK, L.A. Kings ▶▶▶

President's Trophy
(Best Regular-season Record)
VANCOUVER CANUCKS

Hart Trophy (MVP)
EVGENI MALKIN, Pittsburgh Penguins

Vezina Trophy (Best Goaltender)
HENRIK LUNDQVIST, N.Y. Rangers

James Norris Memorial Trophy
(Best Defenseman)
ERIK KARLSSON, Ottawa Senators

Calder Memorial Trophy
(Best Rookie)
GABRIEL LANDESKOG,
Colorado Avalanche

Frank J. Selke Trophy
(Best Defensive Forward)
PATRICE BERGERON, Boston Bruins

Art Ross Trophy (Top Point Scorer)
EVGENI MALKIN, Pittsburgh Penguins

Maurice "Rocket" Richard Trophy
(Top Goal Scorer)
STEVEN STAMKOS, Tampa Bay Lightning

Lady Byng Memorial Trophy
(Most Gentlemanly Player)
◀◀◀**BRIAN CAMPBELL,**
Florida Panthers

Jack Adams Award (Best Coach)
KEN HITCHCOCK, St. Louis Blues

2011-12 Stat Leaders

109 POINTS
Evgeni Malkin, Penguins

60 GOALS
Steven Stamkos, Lightning

67 ASSISTS
Henrik Sedin, Canucks ▶ ▶ ▶

1.56 GOALS AGAINST AVG.
Brian Elliott, Blues

.940 SAVE PERCENTAGE
Brian Elliott, Blues

10 SHUTOUTS
Jonathan Quick, Kings

43 WINS
Pekka Rinne, Predators

+36 PLUS/MINUS
Patrice Bergeron, Bruins

A WORLD RECORD IN 2013?

The NHL might see a world record set on January 1, 2013. The annual Winter Classic outdoor game is set for massive Michigan Stadium. Detroit will take on Toronto in front of what could be more than 120,000 people! The stadium already holds the record from a college game in 2010. The NHL might be an even bigger draw.

WHAT'S NEXT?

Here's our Stanley Cup Finals prediction: The offseason and free agency will bring a lot of teams their missing pieces. We predict the **Los Angeles Kings** will return to the Stanley Cup Final, where they will face another East Coast titan: this time the **New York Rangers**.

Stanley Cup Champions

2011–12	**Los Angeles Kings**		1985–86	**Montreal Canadiens**
2010–11	**Boston Bruins**		1984–85	**Edmonton Oilers**
2009–10	**Chicago Blackhawks**		1983–84	**Edmonton Oilers**
2008–09	**Pittsburgh Penguins**		1982–83	**New York Islanders**
2007–08	**Detroit Red Wings**		1981–82	**New York Islanders**
2006–07	**Anaheim Ducks**		1980–81	**New York Islanders**
2005–06	**Carolina Hurricanes**		1979–80	**New York Islanders**
2004–05	No champion (Lockout)		1978–79	**Montreal Canadiens**
2003–04	**Tampa Bay Lightning**		1977–78	**Montreal Canadiens**
2002–03	**New Jersey Devils**		1976–77	**Montreal Canadiens**
2001–02	**Detroit Red Wings**		1975–76	**Montreal Canadiens**
2000–01	**Colorado Avalanche**		1974–75	**Philadelphia Flyers**
1999–00	**New Jersey Devils**		1973–74	**Philadelphia Flyers**
1998–99	**Dallas Stars**		1972–73	**Montreal Canadiens**
1997–98	**Detroit Red Wings**		1971–72	**Boston Bruins**
1996–97	**Detroit Red Wings**		1970–71	**Montreal Canadiens**
1995–96	**Colorado Avalanche**		1969–70	**Boston Bruins**
1994–95	**New Jersey Devils**		1968–69	**Montreal Canadiens**
1993–94	**New York Rangers**		1967–68	**Montreal Canadiens**
1992–93	**Montreal Canadiens**		1966–67	**Toronto Maple Leafs**
1991–92	**Pittsburgh Penguins**		1965–66	**Montreal Canadiens**
1990–91	**Pittsburgh Penguins**		1964–65	**Montreal Canadiens**
1989–90	**Edmonton Oilers**		1963–64	**Toronto Maple Leafs**
1988–89	**Calgary Flames**		1962–63	**Toronto Maple Leafs**
1987–88	**Edmonton Oilers**		1961–62	**Toronto Maple Leafs**
1986–87	**Edmonton Oilers**		1960–61	**Chicago Blackhawks**

1959–60	**Montreal Canadiens**
1958–59	**Montreal Canadiens**
1957–58	**Montreal Canadiens**
1956–57	**Montreal Canadiens**
1955–56	**Montreal Canadiens**
1954–55	**Detroit Red Wings**
1953–54	**Detroit Red Wings**
1952–53	**Montreal Canadiens**
1951–52	**Detroit Red Wings**
1950–51	**Toronto Maple Leafs**
1949–50	**Detroit Red Wings**
1948–49	**Toronto Maple Leafs**
1947–48	**Toronto Maple Leafs**
1946–47	**Toronto Maple Leafs**
1945–46	**Montreal Canadiens**
1944–45	**Toronto Maple Leafs**
1943–44	**Montreal Canadiens**
1942–43	**Detroit Red Wings**
1941–42	**Toronto Maple Leafs**
1940–41	**Boston Bruins**
1939–40	**New York Rangers**
1938–39	**Boston Bruins**
1937–38	**Chicago Blackhawks**
1936–37	**Detroit Red Wings**
1935–36	**Detroit Red Wings**
1934–35	**Montreal Maroons**
1933–34	**Chicago Blackhawks**
1932–33	**New York Rangers**
1931–32	**Toronto Maple Leafs**

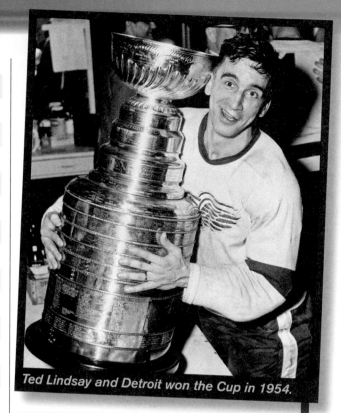

Ted Lindsay and Detroit won the Cup in 1954.

1930–31	**Montreal Canadiens**
1929–30	**Montreal Canadiens**
1928–29	**Boston Bruins**
1927–28	**New York Rangers**
1926–27	**Ottawa Senators**
1925–26	**Montreal Maroons**
1924–25	**Victoria Cougars**
1923–24	**Montreal Canadiens**
1922–23	**Ottawa Senators**
1921–22	**Toronto St. Pats**
1920–21	**Ottawa Senators**
1919–20	**Ottawa Senators**
1918–19	No decision
1917–18	**Toronto Arenas**

NASCAR

WINNER SPINNER!
The most popular driver in NASCAR hasn't been one of its most successful in the past few years. So when Dale Earnhardt Jr. won the Quicken Loans 400 at Michigan International Speedway, he spun out for joy, thrilling his millions of fans. Read more about Earnhardt's success on page 121.

The 2011 Chase

This was one of Stewart's five victories during the Chase.

❝I have to say under the circumstances, I've got to believe this is one of the greatest races of my career.❞

— TONY STEWART

Jimmie Johnson just couldn't win every year, could he? As NASCAR's 2011 Chase for the Cup headed toward the end, it looked like his amazing five-year run as the champ was finally going to end. He was trailing several other drivers heading into the season-ending race in Miami. The big question was, who would be able to pick up where his streak ended?

The result was the closest championship race in NASCAR history.

Entering the 2011 Ford 400 at Homestead Raceway, Tony Stewart and Carl Edwards were neck-and-neck in the points standings. In fact, Edwards, a preseason favorite to dethrone Johnson, was ahead by three points. If Stewart could win the race, that would probably give him enough points to win, however.

So that's just what he did. He and his team gambled and only swapped in two tires on their final pit stop. The seconds that he

Brad Keselowski, out front here, is one of NASCAR's hottest drivers.

saved put him in the lead for good and he held on to win the race. Both he and Edwards ended the season with 2,403 points, the first tie in NASCAR history for the top spot. The tiebreaker? Race wins, and Stewart's five gave him his third NASCAR title and first since 2002.

Few thought Stewart would end up on top when the Chase began. He had not won a single race and was 10th in the Chase standings—but what a finish! In the 10-race Chase series, Stewart won five races! He won the first one and then three of the final four to roar back to the top.

It was one of the most impressive final months by a NASCAR driver ever.

That was not the only news from the 2011 NASCAR season. The five drivers who won their first race was tied for the most since 1970. The winning five: **Trevor Bayne**, **Regan Smith**, **David Ragan**, **Paul Menard**, and **Marcos Ambrose**. In all, 18 different drivers gave their fans a race win in 2011, showing how competitive NASCAR has become.

Brad Keselowski was not a first-time winner in 2011, but it was the first time he won multiple races. He's a driver to watch in the coming years.

Also in 2011, NASCAR had a race on Tuesday for only the second time since 1978. Tropical Storm Lee drenched Georgia in September. The NASCAR race in Atlanta had to be postponed for two days. **Jeff Gordon** won to become only the third NASCAR driver with 85 career victories, joining **Richard Petty** and **David Pearson**.

CHASE FOR THE CUP
2011 FINAL STANDINGS

PLACE/DRIVER	POINTS
1 **Tony STEWART**	2,403
2 **Carl EDWARDS**	2,403
3 **Kevin HARVICK**	2,345
4 **Matt KENSETH**	2,330
5 **Brad KESELOWSKI**	2,319
6 **Jimmie JOHNSON**	2,304
7 **Dale EARNHARDT Jr.**	2,290
8 **Jeff GORDON**	2,287
9 **Denny HAMLIN**	2,284
10 **Ryan NEWMAN**	2,284
11 **Kurt BUSCH**	2,262
12 **Kyle BUSCH**	2,246

Around the Track

Daytona Starts with a Blast! ▶▶▶

The 2012 Daytona 500 was a wild and wacky race. First, a rainstorm moved the race from a Sunday to a Monday evening. The checkered flag didn't drop until nearly 1 A.M. on Tuesday! All the rain didn't prevent a big fireball, however. On Lap 160, while drivers were moving slowly during a yellow-flag caution, Juan Pablo Montoya accidentally hit a truck that was trying to dry the track. The collision ignited the jet fuel used by the truck. A huge fireball rose over the course! The fuel burned for two minutes, and it took two hours to clean the track for a restart. No one

was hurt, but the leader at the time, Dave Blaney, couldn't get back his momentum. The final lap brought more excitement as Matt Kenseth, Greg Biffle, and fan favorite Dale Earnhardt Jr. were neck-and-neck. Kenseth held on to just edge out Earnhardt and wrap up a very weird Daytona 500.

◀◀◀ Bad Boy Busch

Being mean can get you in trouble, on or off the race track. Kurt Busch yelled at a TV reporter after being warned by NASCAR to keep his temper in check. The outburst was one too many and he was suspended from a race in Pennsylvania, costing his team a chance at valuable points.

Yes, That's Him ▲

Believe it or not, that's Jimmie Johnson under that wild wig. He won his third race of the 2012 season and 58th of his great career in June in Delaware. His car was sponsored by a movie, so he and his crew put on these wigs that appeared in the movie. When you win, you can wear anything you want and still look like a champion!

Welcome, Danica! ▲

After teasing her fans for several years, Danica Patrick made it official for 2012. She left Indy cars and joined NASCAR full-time. Driving for Tommy Baldwin Racing, she took part in Nationwide races and a handful of Sprint Cup starts. In 2013, she expects to drive Sprint Cup full-time, so watch out, boys!

Junior Finally Wins

Dale Earnhardt Jr. has been voted by fans as the most popular driver 10 times. He's made the Chase for the Cup several times and finished seventh overall in 2011. But he hadn't won a race for almost four years . . . until June 17, 2012. Earnhardt, son of the late and legendary NASCAR racer whose name he bears, won the Quicken Loans 400 at Michigan International Speedway. The win came, appropriately, on Father's Day.

In the lead with 15 laps to go, Earnhardt said afterward, "I was just thinking, man, those laps could not go by fast enough." The win continued a solid season by the veteran. It was his 15th top-five finish of the year. Many fans hoped he would also come up with his first NASCAR championship in November.

2011 Nationwide Series

Nationwide drivers use cars that are slightly less powerful than Sprint Cup cars. But that doesn't mean the action is not as exciting or the racing any less tense. Nationwide, fans enjoyed a tremendous battle for the championship in 2011. By midseason, several drivers were around the points lead. But in June, **Ricky Stenhouse Jr.** (left) claimed the top spot, and never let it go. He ended 2011 with the most wins (2), the most top 5s (16), and the most top 10s (26) of any driver. He made it even harder for opponents to catch him by earning the most bonus points for leading laps.

At the end of 2010, he was recovering from a bad crash and tough season. Entering 2011, he was hoping to turn things around. He did that and more and credited team owner **Jack Roush** with never giving up on him. Stenhouse's 2011 Nationwide championship makes him a driver to watch in the future.

2011 TRUCK SERIES

The 2011 Camping World Truck Series championship was a family affair. Austin Dillon (right) won the series championship a year after being named rookie of the year. He also was the youngest driver ever to take the title. His proud grandfather, Richard Childress, is one of Dillon's team owners. Childress is a former driver and a winning team owner in Sprint Cup, too. Meanwhile, Austin's brother Ty was the 2011 ARCA Series champion.

Austin was consistent all season. His series-best 16 top-10 finishes included a pair of victories.

Also in the Truck Series, another Busch got in trouble in November. Kyle Busch smacked into Ron Hornaday on purpose during a race in Texas. Hornaday was okay, but his truck was ruined. Race officials pulled Busch off the track. He was also kept out of Sunday's car races and fined.

Jimmie at Indy! ▲

For the fourth time, Jimmie Johnson kissed the bricks at Indy. It's gross, but for racers, it's an honor. The Indianapolis Motor Speedway used to be paved with bricks, so it's called The Brickyard. There is one strip of them left on the track. After a win, the driver kisses the bricks in thanks.

Cursed?

No one likes to finish second in a NASCAR race. Now it looks like finishing second in the season standings is bad news, too. Carl Edwards was the runner-up in 2011, but had a terrible 2012 season with no wins through July. In 2011, Denny Hamlin also had a rough year after finishing second in 2010. And Mark Martin (2009) and Edwards himself (2008) also struggled after earning NASCAR's version of a silver medal. Are NASCAR runners-up cursed? Stay tuned for the 2013 season to see if the curse continues!

2013: NEW SPRINT CUP CAR

In 2013, NASCAR racers will look more like a car your family might drive. NASCAR announced that Sprint Cup teams will use one of four new body shapes in 2013: Chevrolet SS, Ford Fusion, Dodge Charger, or Toyota Camry.

The engines will be the same, but the exteriors will change. Team owners and designers have been working to get the cars ready. "The final product will be head and shoulders [above] where we've been last few years," said NASCAR vice president Robin Pemberton.

2012 NASCAR CHAMPION

Last year in this space, we wrote that Jimmie Johnson would not win his sixth title. We got that right, but we got the winner wrong—but we'll keep trying. The 2012 NASCAR champion will (we think . . .) be:

★ Dale Earnhardt Jr. ★

NASCAR Champions

Year	Driver	Make		Year	Driver	Make
2011	Tony Stewart	Chevrolet		1992	Alan Kulwicki	Ford
2010	Jimmie Johnson	Chevrolet		1991	Dale Earnhardt Sr.	Chevrolet
2009	Jimmie Johnson	Chevrolet		1990	Dale Earnhardt Sr.	Chevrolet
2008	Jimmie Johnson	Chevrolet		1989	Rusty Wallace	Pontiac
2007	Jimmie Johnson	Chevrolet		1988	Bill Elliott	Ford
2006	Jimmie Johnson	Chevrolet		1987	Dale Earnhardt Sr.	Chevrolet
2005	Tony Stewart	Chevrolet		1986	Dale Earnhardt Sr.	Chevrolet
2004	Kurt Busch	Ford		1985	Darrell Waltrip	Chevrolet
2003	Matt Kenseth	Ford		1984	Terry Labonte	Chevrolet
2002	Tony Stewart	Pontiac		1983	Bobby Allison	Buick
2001	Jeff Gordon	Chevrolet		1982	Darrell Waltrip	Buick
2000	Bobby Labonte	Pontiac		1981	Darrell Waltrip	Buick
1999	Dale Jarrett	Ford		1980	Dale Earnhardt Sr.	Chevrolet
1998	Jeff Gordon	Chevrolet		1979	Richard Petty	Chevrolet
1997	Jeff Gordon	Chevrolet		1978	Cale Yarborough	Oldsmobile
1996	Terry Labonte	Chevrolet		1977	Cale Yarborough	Chevrolet
1995	Jeff Gordon	Chevrolet		1976	Cale Yarborough	Chevrolet
1994	Dale Earnhardt Sr.	Chevrolet		1975	Richard Petty	Dodge
1993	Dale Earnhardt Sr.	Chevrolet		1974	Richard Petty	Dodge

1973	Benny Parsons	Chevrolet
1972	Richard Petty	Plymouth
1971	Richard Petty	Plymouth
1970	Bobby Isaac	Dodge
1969	David Pearson	Ford
1968	David Pearson	Ford
1967	Richard Petty	Plymouth
1966	David Pearson	Dodge
1965	Ned Jarrett	Ford
1964	Richard Petty	Plymouth
1963	Joe Weatherly	Pontiac
1962	Joe Weatherly	Pontiac
1961	Ned Jarrett	Chevrolet

1960	Rex White	Chevrolet
1959	Lee Petty	Plymouth
1958	Lee Petty	Oldsmobile
1957	Buck Baker	Chevrolet
1956	Buck Baker	Chrysler
1955	Tim Flock	Chrysler
1954	Lee Petty	Chrysler
1953	Herb Thomas	Hudson
1952	Tim Flock	Hudson
1951	Herb Thomas	Hudson
1950	Bill Rexford	Oldsmobile
1949	Red Byron	Oldsmobile

NASCAR'S WINNINGEST DRIVERS

(career Cup series victories entering 2012)

DRIVER	RACES WON	DRIVER	RACES WON
1. Richard PETTY	200	6. Jeff GORDON	82
2. David PEARSON	105	7. Dale EARNHARDT Sr.	76
3. Bobby ALLISON	84	8. Rusty WALLACE	55
Darrell WALTRIP	84	9. Jimmie JOHNSON	54
5. Cale YARBOROUGH	83	Lee PETTY	54

OTHER MOTOR SPORTS

HIGH FLYER!

Motorcycle superstar Ryan Dungey gets some big air while competing in AMASupercross in St. Louis. Dungey dominated the indoor racing season after finishing second in the outdoor Motocross events. He's got a long way to go to catch the great Ricky Carmichael, but Dungey is off to a rip-roaring start. Read more about both seasons on page 133.

Formula 1

Back-to-Back!

In 2011, **Sebastian Vettel** became the youngest driver ever to win back-to-back Formula 1 championships. He set an all-time record by capturing 15 pole positions. He went on to win 11 races and had the title sewn up before the final race was even run. Vettel was so dominant that he finished second in four other races, and never finished lower than fourth (except for one race he did not finish).

Born in Germany, Vettel got his start in racing on the popular karting tracks in Europe. Vettel won 18 out of 20 races in the series one below Formula 1, when he was only 17. He showed he belonged with the big boys just a few years later, and now with two world championships is the brightest light on the circuit.

Another young driver, **Lewis Hamilton** of England, was the 2010 champion; he won three races in 2011. The 2009 champ, **Jenson Button**, also won a trio of races.

2011 F1 FINAL STANDINGS

PLACE/DRIVER	POINTS
1. Sebastian Vettel	392
2. Jenson Button	270
3. Mark Webber	258
4. Fernando Alonso	257
5. Lewis Hamilton	227

2011 FORMULA 1 HIGHLIGHTS

RACE OF THE YEAR ▶▶▶

Jenson Button put on a show in the rain at the event in Montreal, Canada. The conditions were tough for the racers and the race was stopped for two hours while the heaviest rain fell. Button got a penalty for speeding on a caution lap. After the rain delay, he had to start from the back of the pack, but passed driver after driver. He slid by **Vettel** on the final lap for an amazing victory.

FIRST FORMULA 1 IN INDIA

Formula 1 is the most international racing circuit, with its globe-trotting drivers spending more time in planes than their fast-moving cars. In October 2011, India welcomed its first F1 race, held near New Delhi. **Sebastian Vettel** took the pole and then the victory. A local hero was **Narain Karthikeyan**, the only native Indian in the field. Unfortunately, after a crash, he finished 17th.

2012 F1 NEWS

Tough Competition

While **Sebastian Vettel** goes for his third straight title, he'll have to get past an amazing field of drivers. Among the 24 drivers who started the 2012 season, six, including Vettel, have won at least one world championship.

A Crazy Start ▶▶▶

In 2012, six different drivers won races in the first six races of the season. The biggest surprise was **Pastor Maldonado**, who won the race in Spain. He was the first driver from Venezuela to earn a Formula 1 victory.

How Do You Say "Yee-Haw!" in German?

A racing circuit that already includes such exotic places as Kuala Lumpur, Singapore, and Monte Carlo added a new racing home in November 2012: Texas! At the new Circuit of the Americas near Austin, F1 racing returns to the U.S. for the first time since 2007.

IndyCar

Franchitti and his team were on target for another Indy title.

Other highlights of the 2011 season included:

➤ A trip to Brazil for a race in São Paulo.

➤ The first win in five years for **Marco Andretti** of the famous racing family.

➤ A race in Edmonton, Canada, that was laid out in a place used to high speeds—the city airport's runways.

➤ IndyCar's first visit to Baltimore, where the race was held on blocked-off city streets.

"Timing is everything," goes the old saying. In the 2011 IndyCar season, **Dario Franchitti** proved it's still true. For the third season in a row, the Scottish driver with the Italian name took over the season points lead in the last possible race. Franchitti won only four races compared to runner-up **Will Power**'s six. But in Kentucky in the last race that counted, Franchitti finished second while Power dropped way back. That gave Franchitti enough points to earn his third straight crown.

Also, the September race in Japan was nearly called off in the aftermath of the tsunami that hit that country in March. However, local organizers worked to get things ready so that Japanese fans could enjoy one of their favorite sports.

In 2012, the season got off to a "Power-ful" start. Will Power won three of the season's first four races to jump out to a big lead in points. The other big early news was the departure of **Danica Patrick** to

SAD NEWS The final race of the 2011 season ended early for a tragic reason. Popular driver and former champion **Dan Wheldon** was killed in a multicar wreck at the event in Las Vegas. The accident happened very early in the race, which was immediately canceled. The crash was a reminder that the sport, while thrilling, can also be dangerous.

2012 INDY 500

In the 2011 Indy 500, a driver made a crucial error on the final lap and ended up losing a race he should have won. In 2012, another driver, **Takuma Sato**, tried something similar. Sato was not in the lead, but he tried for a daring inside pass on leader **Dario Franchitti**. It didn't work. Sato spun his car and crashed into the wall. Franchitti held on for his third Indy 500 victory.

On a hot day in Indianapolis, it was a record-setting race. Drivers changed the lead 35 times, the most ever in a race first run back in 1911. There was also only one crash, which meant that drivers were at top speed more often. The day was emotional, too. It was the first Indy 500 since the death of 2011 winner **Dan Wheldon** (see box).

The win put the Scottish driver with the Italian name in elite company (below). Just like we noted about his 2011 season victory . . . timing is everything.

To the winner goes the milk!

NASCAR. The only top woman driver in IndyCar, losing Patrick could mean a few less headlines for IndyCar in 2012.

Another American driver was making news in 2012, however. In June, **Ryan Hunter-Reay** won in Toronto. It was his third straight race win, the best by a driver from the U.S. since 2006. With more American IndyCar drivers than usual in 2012, was this the year the trophy stayed home?

2011 IZOD INDYCAR SERIES FINAL STANDINGS

PLACE/DRIVER	POINTS
1. Dario Franchitti	573
2. Will Power	555
3. Scott Dixon	518
4. Oriol Servia	425
5. Tony Kanaan	366

Most Indy 500 Wins
(ALL-TIME)

4 A. J. Foyt (pictured), Al Unser, Rick Mears

3 Louis Meyer, Wilbur Shaw, Mauri Rose, Johnny Rutherford, Bobby Unser, Helio Castroneves, Dario Franchitti

2011 NHRA

Drag racing continues to draw fans of high-speed vehicles. The mighty roar of their engines means you can't go to a race without ear protection! And although the races are over in seconds, the thrills of seeing cars reach more than 300 miles per hour last forever.

In 2011, the National Hot Rod Association's four main racing series saw two new champions and a pair of repeat winners.

TOP FUEL: Del Worsham spent 20 years driving Funny Cars. Moving up to the Top Fuel division, he found instant success, winning his first championship. He won eight races in the season, including the big final race at Pomona, California. A thrilling semifinal matchup between Worsham and

2011 NHRA FINAL STANDINGS

Top Fuel	Del Worsham
Funny Car	Matt Hagan
Pro Stock	Jason Line
Pro Stock Motorcycle	Eddie Krawiec

Spencer Massey was the difference. Worsham won by .008 seconds.

FUNNY CAR: In 2010, **Matt Hagan** thought he had his first title sewn up. He entered the last day of racing with a 38-point lead. But he ended up in second place overall after champion **John Force** overtook him. In 2011, Hagan made sure history did not repeat. He set a new national record with a 3.995-second run and clinched his first title.

PRO STOCK: Jason Line had been a champion before, but that came all the way back in 2006. He racked up enough points in 2011 to lock up his second title two weeks before the end of the season.

PRO STOCK MOTORCYCLE: Eddie Krawiec won his first title in 2008, but he won it without winning a race—he just piled up points. In 2011, however, he did both—he won four races and made six final pairings to capture the season championship.

There was nothing funny about how fast Matt Hagan drove in 2011.

Motocross/Supercross

2011 AMA Motocross

A rider named Ryan once again was the AMA Motocross champion in 2011. However, it was not defending champ **Ryan Dungey**, but **Ryan Villopoto** who swept into the title. The veteran rider racked up 526 season points, just ahead of Dungey.

What makes the victory so impressive is that Villopoto had to come back from a 2010 crash. In that accident, he broke his ankle and two bones in his leg. It was a long and hard road back, but he battled and won three races in 2011 on his way to his second—and sweetest—season championship.

V for Villopoto . . . and victory!

2012 AMA Supercross

The indoor racing season once again saw the battle of the Ryans. As the series moved around the country, filling stadiums with cheering fans, **Villopoto** and **Dungey** were once again the favorites to capture the title. Dungey had won it all in 2011 while Villopoto was coming off his championship outdoor season.

On the stadium courses, though, Dungey was supreme. He regularly finished among the top three racers and racked up enough points to finish ahead of Villopoto and former champion **James Stewart Jr.**

For the 2012 season, Dungey and Stewart changed teams, with Stewart taking over Dungey's role with Suzuki and Dungey joining the new Red Bull team. The former training partners are sure to have tough battles on the track! Villopoto, however, was out for the 2012 season with a knee injury.

WORLD CHAMPS!

Motocross is usually an individual sport. Racers battle each other to come out on top. But at the Motocross des Nations (Motocross of Nations), it's country vs. country. Teams of three riders represent their native lands in a series of races. In 2011, the U.S. team of **Ryan Villopoto**, **Ryan Dungey**, and **Blake Baggett** (pictured) rode to glory. They finished ahead of France.

Major Champions
OF THE 2000s

TOP FUEL DRAGSTERS

YEAR	DRIVER
2011	Del Worsham
2010	Larry Dixon
2009	Tony Schumacher
2008	Tony Schumacher
2007	Tony Schumacher
2006	Tony Schumacher
2005	Tony Schumacher
2004	Tony Schumacher
2003	Larry Dixon
2002	Larry Dixon
2001	Kenny Bernstein
2000	Gary Scelzi

FUNNY CARS

YEAR	DRIVER
2011	Matt Hagan
2010	John Force
2009	Robert Hight
2008	Cruz Pedregon
2007	Tony Pedregon
2006	John Force
2005	Gary Scelzi
2004	John Force
2003	Tony Pedregon
2002	John Force
2001	John Force
2000	John Force

PRO STOCK CARS

YEAR	DRIVER
2011	Jason Line
2010	Greg Anderson
2009	Mike Edwards
2008	Jeg Coughlin Jr.
2007	Jeg Coughlin Jr.
2006	Jason Line
2005	Greg Anderson
2004	Greg Anderson
2003	Greg Anderson
2002	Jeg Coughlin Jr.
2001	Warren Johnson
2000	Jeg Coughlin Jr.

FORMULA ONE

YEAR	DRIVER
2011	Sebastian Vettel
2010	Sebastian Vettel
2009	Jenson Button
2008	Lewis Hamilton
2007	Kimi Räikkönen
2006	Fernando Alonso
2005	Fernando Alonso
2004	Michael Schumacher
2003	Michael Schumacher
2002	Michael Schumacher
2001	Michael Schumacher
2000	Michael Schumacher

INDYCAR SERIES

YEAR	DRIVER
2011	**Dario Franchitti**
2010	**Dario Franchitti**
2009	**Dario Franchitti**
2008	**Scott Dixon**
2007	**Dario Franchitti**
2006	**Sam Hornish Jr. and Dan Wheldon (tie)**
2005	**Dan Wheldon**
2004	**Tony Kanaan**
2003	**Scott Dixon**
2002	**Sam Hornish Jr.**
2001	**Sam Hornish Jr.**
2000	**Buddy Lazier**

AMA SUPERCROSS

YEAR	DRIVER
2012	**Ryan Dungey**
2011	**Ryan Villopoto**
2010	**Ryan Dungey**
2009	**James Stewart Jr.**
2008	**Chad Reed**
2007	**James Stewart Jr.**
2006	**Ricky Carmichael**
2005	**Ricky Carmichael**
2004	**Chad Reed**
2003	**Ricky Carmichael**
2002	**Ricky Carmichael**
2001	**Ricky Carmichael**
2000	**Jeremy McGrath**

AMA MOTOCROSS

YEAR	RIDER (MOTOCROSS)	RIDER (LITES)
2011	**Ryan Villopoto**	**Dean Wilson**
2010	**Ryan Dungey**	**Trey Canard**
2009	**Chad Reed**	**Ryan Dungey**
2008	**James Stewart Jr.**	**Ryan Villopoto**
2007	**Grant Langston**	**Ryan Villopoto**
2006	**Ricky Carmichael**	**Ryan Villopoto**
2005	**Ricky Carmichael**	**Ivan Tedesco**
2004	**Ricky Carmichael**	**James Stewart Jr.**
2003	**Ricky Carmichael**	**Grant Langston**
2002	**Ricky Carmichael**	**James Stewart Jr.**
2001	**Ricky Carmichael**	**Mike Brown**
2000	**Ricky Carmichael**	**Travis Pastrana**

Dean Wilson

ACTION SPORTS

SWEET SPOT
American **Kelly Slater** ducks down under the curl in an Association of Surfing Professionals (ASP) event at Ocean Beach in San Francisco. The surfing legend won his record 11th ASP men's world championship in the 2011 season (see page 138).

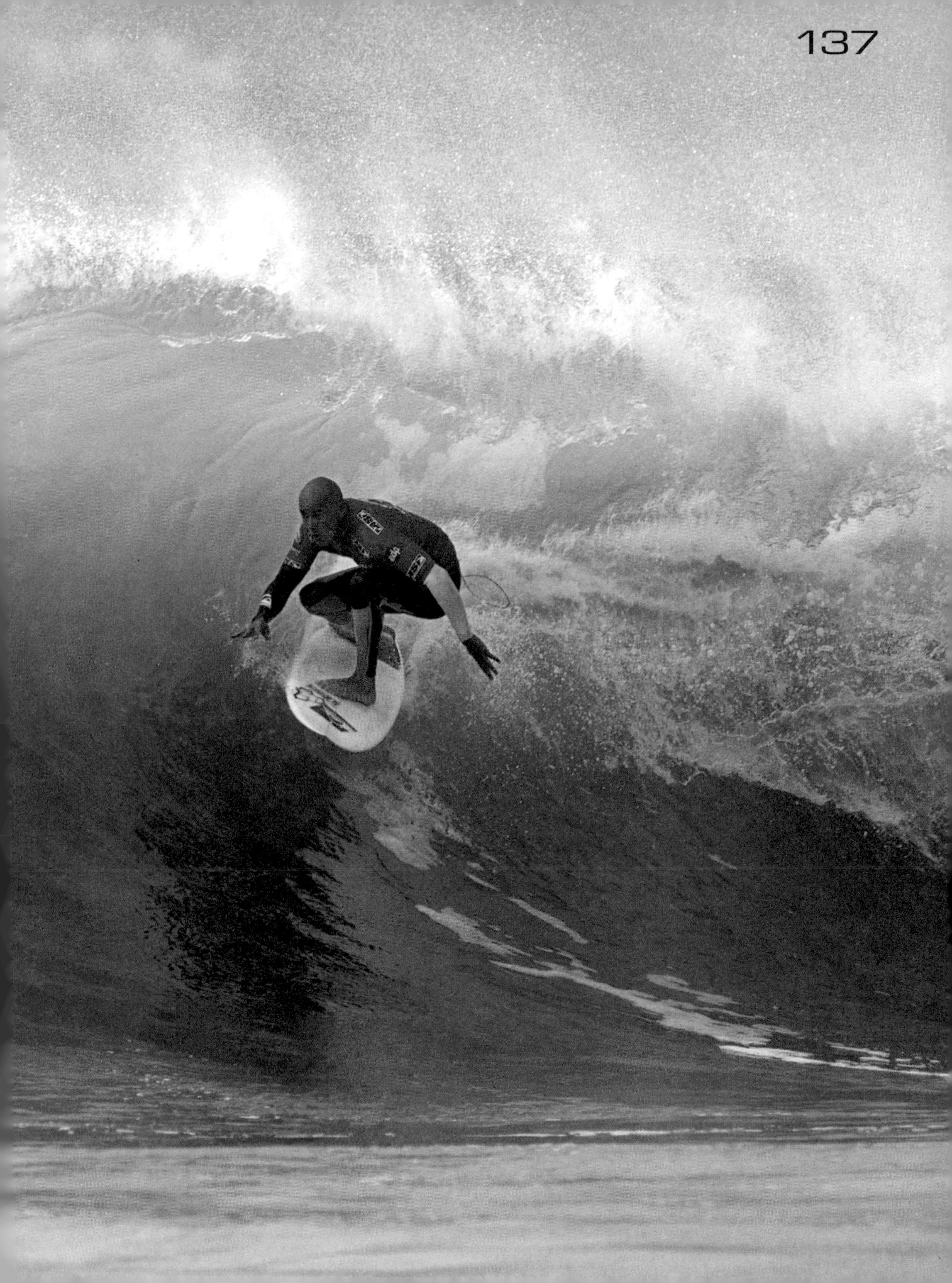

2011-2012 Wrap-up

11s Are Wild

In 2011, surfing legend **Kelly Slater** turned 39 years old on February 11—or 2/11 on the calendar. Nearly nine months later, on November 2—or 11/2 on the calendar—he won his 11th Association of Surfing Professionals (ASP) world championship. "It's a weird coincidence and it does feel like the completion of something," Slater said.

Slater clinched the title during the opening heats of the 2011 Rip Curl Pro Search in San Francisco. The rest of that event and another in Hawaii were still on the schedule, but he was too far ahead for anyone to catch.

Are there still more titles in Slater's future? "I honestly don't think about twelve," he said after winning No. 11. But don't

Carissa Moore of Hawaii was the top surfer in 2011.

count him out. Despite missing the third event in 2012 due to injury, he was second in the ASP season standings entering the summer. Two-time champ **Mick Fanning** of Australia was in first place.

On the women's side, Australia's **Stephanie Gilmore** won two of the season's first three events to soar to the top of the standings in 2012. Gilmore was trying to reclaim the title after her string of four championships in a row was ended by 18-year-old Hawaiian **Carissa Moore** in 2011.

◀◀◀ Double Fun

It's become a tradition for an action-sports star to pull off an incredible feat for the

DEW TOUR 2011–2012

WINTER

CHAMPION	EVENT
Nick Goepper	FREESKI SLOPESTYLE
Kaya Turski	WOMEN'S FREESKI SLOPESTYLE
David Wise	FREESKI SUPERPIPE
Devin Logan	WOMEN'S FREESKI SUPERPIPE
Sebastien Toutant	SNOWBOARD SLOPESTYLE
Spencer O'Brien	WOMEN'S SNOWBOARD SLOPESTYLE
Louie Vito	SNOWBOARD SUPERPIPE
Kelly Clark	WOMEN'S SNOWBOARD SUPERPIPE

SUMMER

CHAMPION	EVENT
Dennis Enarson	BMX DIRT
Scotty Cranmer	BMX PARK
Jamie Bestwick	BMX VERT
Ryan Decenzo	SKATE STREET
Pierre-Luc Gagnon	SKATE VERT

New Year. The annual Red Bull No Limits stunt was twice as fun in 2012, when **Levi LaVallee** (snowmobile) and **Robbie Maddison** (motorcycle) pulled it off together. They did a tandem jump over the San Diego marina on December 31, 2011. In previous years, Maddison had performed stunts like leaping 100 feet to the top of a Las Vegas hotel or soaring over the Corinth Canal in Greece.

LaVallee and Maddison both easily cleared the gap in San Diego. They hit the landing ramp hard, but stayed with their vehicles. Which flies farther: a 450-pound snowmobile or a 245-pound motorcycle? It was LaVallee and the snowmobile, at 412 feet 6 inches. Maddison went 378 feet 9 inches on his motorcycle. Both riders broke world records for their vehicles.

Endurocross

Poland's **Taddy Blazusiak** has been the world's best Endurocross rider for several years now. (Endurocross combines the excitement of supercross with the uncertainty of trail riding.) Blazusiak's performance in 2011 was extreme, though, even by his standards.

Blazusiak started the year off by winning the first Enduro X competition at the X Games, which counts in the Endurocross

season standings. Then he won again . . . over and over! In eight main events, Blazusiak won seven times. He won the season championship (his third in a row) in a rout.

Surprisingly, though, Blazusiak was just fourth in Enduro X at the X Games in 2012. **Mike Brown** won it. Still, Blazusiak was in first place in the season standings almost halfway into the season schedule.

Blazusiak dominates in the grueling Endurocross.

Winter X Games

Shaun White added another record to his amazing career.

JUST PERFECT

Shaun White won the men's Snowboard SuperPipe at the Winter X Games in Aspen, Colorado, in 2012. But White pretty much always takes home the gold in his signature event.

Even for White, who won the event for the fifth year in a row, this one was special. With his 12th career Winter X Games gold already wrapped up, White made his victory run memorable. He unveiled a front-side double cork 1260 to earn a 100 score from the judges. It was the first perfect score in Winter X Games history. "It's unreal," he said. "I've been wanting that 100 forever."

It didn't look like this would be the year. White almost had to pull out of the SuperPipe because of a sprained ankle.

With his gold medal, White joined **Nate Holland** (in Snowboarder X) and **Tucker Hibbert** (Snowmobile Snocross) as the only athletes to five-peat in the Winter X Games.

In Memory of Sarah

These X Games were dedicated to skier **Sarah Burke**. The 2011 champion in the women's Ski SuperPipe, Burke died just one week before the start of the Winter X Games 16. While practicing on the halfpipe in Park City, Utah, she fell on her head after completing a trick, and later went into cardiac arrest. On opening night of the X Games, the superpipe was darkened in memory of Burke. Family, friends, and competitors held a candlelight vigil at the top.

FLIPPED OUT

If it can be done on a motorcycle, why not on a snowmobile? That's what **Heath Frisby** thought after seeing **Jackson Strong** throw down the first front flip in X Games history to win the Moto X Best Trick competition in the summer of 2011.

So Frisby quietly worked on a front flip on his snowmobile ahead of the 2012 Winter X Games. Few people knew of his plans until he told his Facebook fans the day of the Best Trick event. Frisby nailed it and took home the gold.

SECOND TIME'S THE CHARM

In his first X Games in 2011, teenager **Mark McMorris** finished second in the Snowboard Slopestyle and fourth in Snowboard Big Air. Turns out he was just getting warmed up. In 2012, the 18-year-old Canadian won both of those events in Winter X Games 16.

McMorris already had the gold wrapped up before his third and final run in the Slopestyle. His win in Big Air was more dramatic, though. Norway's **Torstein Horgmo** posted a perfect score on one of his tricks. (The top two tricks are combined for the winning score.) But McMorris nailed the first backside triple cork 1440 in the X Games to earn the gold.

NEWS AND NOTES

Kelly Clark remained unbeatable in the Snowboard SuperPipe. She won for the fourth time at the X Games, and for the 13th time in a row in all competitions dating to 2010. **Colten Moore** won the Snowmobile Freestyle competition. His older brother, **Caleb**, was third in the same event. In the Ski Slopestyle, **Kaya Turski** became the first woman to nail a switch 1080 in the Winter X Games. That enabled her to come from behind and win her third consecutive gold in the event.

Kelly Clark has been unbeatable in Snowboard SuperPipe.

Summer X Games

But Bob Burnquist, 35, ended up as the Big Air winner.

Six-Peat

Like Bob Burnquist in Skate Big Air, **Jamie Bestwick** keeps on holding off the younger guys in BMX Vert. Forty-year-old Bestwick won his sixth consecutive X Games gold in that event.

It wasn't even close, either. Bestwick posted the two best scores of the event. He easily beat **Vince Byron**, who finished in second place.

Bestwick has been so good for so long, he's even started recycling some old moves. "The flair double whip, I haven't done that since the 2005 Best Trick at X Games," he said. But he also admitted he's got some new tricks in reserve—just in case any of the young guys start to catch up.

One for the Old Guys

Five years after **Jake Brown** landed the first 720 in Big Air at the X Games, the 900 barrier was shattered in 2012. Fifteen-year-old **Mitchie Brusco** and 12-year-old **Tom Schaar** worked their way into the final with the historic move. It was **Bob Burnquist**, though, who went on to win the event. At 35, Burnquist is practically an old man compared to the youngsters! But in the final, Burnquist followed a switch backside 180 ollie with a forward-to-fakie grab 720 to win his fourth career gold in Big Air. Brusco finished second, while Schaar was sixth.

Mitchie Brusco, 15, made the Big Air final.

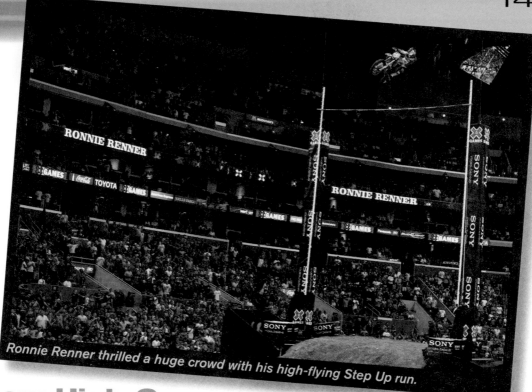

Ronnie Renner thrilled a huge crowd with his high-flying Step Up run.

How High Can They Go?

Ronnie Renner ended **Matt Buyten**'s two-year run as champ of Moto X Step Up—and he did it in record-setting fashion. Buyten set the X Games record when he soared 37 feet to win Step Up in 2011. The two rivals pushed the bar well past that mark in 2012. Renner finally won when he cleared 47 feet.

❝We're falling four stories out of the sky, and that's not talking it up at all. That's being nice. It's pretty gnarly.❞

—RONNIE RENNER, AFTER WINNING THE STEP UP COMPETITION AT A RECORD 47 FEET

Still the One

The BMX Street competition was held for the fifth time at the Summer X Games. Also for the fifth time, **Garrett Reynolds** took home the gold.

There was some suspense to the outcome this time, though. Eighteen-year-old **Chad Kerley** looked like he might end Reynolds's run. Garrett entered the final run of the event needing 42 points to come from behind and win. He got 43 to keep his streak alive.

News and Notes

Vicki Golden led from start to finish to win women's Moto X Racing for the second year in a row. . . . Veteran star **Travis Pastrana** wasn't seen much in these X Games. He competed in RallyCross, but was slammed into the wall on the first turn of the first heat. His car was totaled. . . . **Pierre-Luc Gagnon** of Canada won Skate Vert on a tiebreaker over **Bucky Lasek**. It was PLG's sixth career gold.

2012 X Game Winners

Jamie Anderson's moves earned gold in Snowboard Slopestyle.

Snowboard Big Air
Mark McMorris

Snowboard Slopestyle (Men)
Mark McMorris

Snowboard Slopestyle (Women)
Jamie Anderson

Snowboard Snowboarder X (Men)
Nate Holland

Snowboard Snowboarder X (Women)
Dominique Maltais

Snowboard Street
Forest Bailey

Snowboard SuperPipe (Men)
Shaun White

Snowboard SuperPipe (Women)
Kelly Clark

Snowmobile Best Trick
Heath Frisby

Snowmobile Freestyle
Colten Moore

WINTER X GAMES 16 • Aspen, Colorado
January 26–29, 2012

Skiing Big Air
Bobby Brown

Skiing Mono Skier X
Samson Danniels

Skiing Skier X (Men)
Chris Del Bosco

Skiing Skier X (Women)
Marte Gjefsen

Skiing Slopestyle (Men)
Tom Wallisch

Skiing Slopestyle (Women)
Kaya Turski

Skiing SuperPipe (Men)
David Wise

Skiing SuperPipe (Women)
Roz Groenewoud

SUMMER X GAMES 18 • Los Angeles, California
June 28–July 1, 2012

BMX Big Air
Steve McCann

BMX Street
Garrett Reynolds

BMX Park
Scotty Cranmer

BMX Vert
Jamie Bestwick

Moto X Best Trick
Jackson Strong

Moto X Enduro X (Men)
Mike Brown

Moto X Enduro X (Women)
Maria Forsberg

Moto X Freestyle
Taka Higashino

Moto X Speed & Style
Mike Mason

Moto X Step Up
Ronnie Renner

Moto X Racing (Women)
Vicki Golden

Rally Car RallyCross
Sebastien Loeb

Skate Big Air
Bob Burnquist

Skate Game of SK8
Ryan Decenzo

Skate Park
Pedro Barros

Skate Street (Men)
Paul Rodriguez

Skate Street (Women)
Alexis Sablone

Skate Vert (Men)
Pierre-Luc Gagnon

Taka Higashino soared in Freestyle.

SIX TIMES X

Can't get enough of the X Games? Well, it's not just Aspen in winter and Los Angeles in summer, anymore. Already, the X Games has held competitions in Europe and Asia in recent years. In 2013, it expands to six events—two winter and four summer—around the globe. X Games organizers hope these competitions become the most-talked-about events of the action-sports year, sort of like the "major" championships in golf and tennis.

JANUARY 24–27	Aspen, Colorado
MARCH 20–22	Tignes, France
APRIL 18–21	Foz do Iguaçu, Brazil
MAY 9–12	Barcelona, Spain
JUNE 27–30	Munich, Germany
AUGUST 1–4	Los Angeles, California

SOCCER

GOAAAALLL!
Spain's Fernando Torres watches his shot slide by Italian goalie Gianluigi Buffon in the 2012 European Championship final. Spain dominated the tournament and the game, capturing its third straight major international title.

¡Viva España!

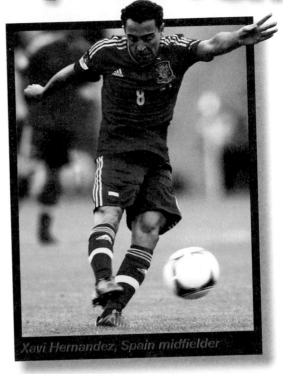

Xavi Hernandez, Spain midfielder

The European Championship of soccer is considered the second-most important contest in the sport behind the World Cup. In the summer of 2012, a champion emerged that is now considered by experts the greatest team of all time: Spain.

Spain defeated Italy, 4–0, in the final game to complete a historic run. Spain won the previous Euro event in 2008, then won the World Cup in 2010. With this repeat in Euro 2012, they became the first nation ever to go back-to-back-to-back like that.

Why has Spain become so dominant? It's a combination of talent and technique. They have very, very skilled players. But the team uses a passing-heavy style of play that is very hard to defend against. Spain makes long series of quick, often one-touch passes in a long string toward a shot. That helps them score, of course, but if you control the ball, the other team can't score either. During the European championships, Spain not only played beautiful soccer, but they also played stingy defense. In fact, they have not given up a goal in a game they had to win since 2008. It also helps that they have a player considered the best goalie in the world, team captain **Iker Casillas**.

Most of the Spanish team plays for the Spanish pro clubs Barcelona and Real Madrid. They are archrivals when they play for their clubs, but join flawlessly for the national team. The top Spanish players include midfielders **Xavi Hernandez**, **Andres Iniesta**, and **Xabi Alonso**. The key defender is **Gerard Pique**. Up front, the team often relies on **Cesc Fabregas** and **Fernando Torres**. Torres won the Golden Boot as the Euro 2012's top scorer.

EUROPEAN CHAMPIONSHIP
FINAL-ROUND
QUARTERFINALS

Portugal 1—Czech Rep. 0
Germany 4—Greece 2
Spain 2—France 0
Italy 0—England 0
(Italy on PKs: 4–2)

SEMIFINALS

Italy 2—Germany 1
Spain 0—Portugal 0
(Spain on PKs: 4–2)

CHAMPIONSHIP GAME

Spain 4—Italy 0

World Soccer

EUROPE'S TOP CLUB

In the European championships, held every four years, national soccer teams play each other, country against country. Every year, however, another popular tournament pits Europe's top pro club teams head-to-head. The UEFA Champions League attracts world attention. Players from all over the globe play in European leagues, and the best teams in those leagues take part in the Champions League.

In 2012, the Champions League finals featured the top players in the world . . . and a surprising result. Most fans hoped for a final that would feature Real Madrid against Barcelona. Those top Spanish teams feature the world's two best players, **Cristiano Ronaldo** and **Lionel Messi** (see box).

In the semifinals, however, both players could not lead their teams to wins.

Facing Chelsea from England's Premier League, Messi and Barcelona were shocked to lose at home. In the second of the two-game semifinals, the great Messi actually missed a penalty kick! In the other semi, it came down to penalty kicks after a two-game tie. In the shootout, Ronaldo's kick was saved by the Bayern Munich goalie! That two such great players both missed penalties was a stunner!

In the final, another great player rose to the occasion. Chelsea's **Didier Drogba** headed in a game-tying goal in the 88th minute. In the penalty-kick shootout, his goal gave the Blues the surprising victory.

Drogba pounded in this penalty kick past Bayern Munich's Manuel Neuer to clinch the title.

WHO'S NO. 1?

Soccer fans debate which player is the best in the world, but they all agree that there are only two choices: **Lionel Messi** (right), who plays for Barcelona and Argentina and **Cristiano Ronaldo**, who plays for Barcelona and Portugal.

Both players had amazing 2011–12 seasons, chasing the Spanish league record and helping their national teams to big wins.

Messi scored 73 goals for his club team, a new single-season record, including 14 in Champions League games. Ronaldo was just behind with 60 total goals, and he led Real Madrid to the Spanish league title.

Messi's talents are dribbling and speed, leading to dozens of shots. Ronaldo is taller and better in the air, but also has great dribbling skills and a nose for the goal. Who's better? It doesn't really matter as long as we all get to watch them play.

WOMEN'S SOCCER

It was a tough year for women's soccer in the U.S. The national team was coming off its disappointment at losing to Japan in the 2011 Women's World Cup. In the annual Algarve Cup, a major event held in Portugal, Japan won again, 1–0, on a goal in the 84th minute. The disappointed U.S. team got out its frustration on Sweden in the third-place game. **Alex Morgan** had a hat trick in the 4–0 rout.

The other tough news for women's soccer was the end of another pro league. Women's Professional Soccer (WPS) closed in early 2012 after three seasons. Not enough people watched the games and TV money was not available, so WPS could not survive.

Alex Morgan scored three goals against Sweden.

MLS Report

Galaxy Wins!

The MLS Cup is held at a different stadium each year. It's picked at least a year in advance, but every team hopes that they get the home-field advantage. In 2011, it was the Los Angeles Galaxy who played host to the MLS Cup . . . and they enjoyed support from a sell-out crowd at L.A.'s Home Depot Center. Featuring stars **Landon Donovan**, **David Beckham**, and **Robbie Keane**, the Galaxy buzzed through the regular season. They were regarded as one of MLS's best teams, with the second-most points in a season ever. However, they had to come through with a title to clinch it.

In MLS Cup 2011, they faced the Houston Dymano, an upset winner in the semifinals over favored Sporting KC.

A little rain didn't bother the fans who packed Home Depot Center for the MLS Cup. Both teams had

2011 MLS AWARDS

MVP: **Dwayne De Rosario**, D.C. UNITED

GOLDEN BOOT: **De Rosario**

ROOKIE OF THE YEAR:
C.J. Sapong, SPORTING KC

DEFENDER OF THE YEAR:
Omar Gonzalez, LOS ANGELES GALAXY

COMEBACK PLAYER OF THE YEAR:
David Beckham, LOS ANGELES GALAXY

WINNERS XBOX 360 TEAM FAIR PLAY:
Portland Timbers

good chances in the first half, but no goals appeared. Beckham thrilled fans when he bent one of his famous free kicks just over the bar.

In the second half, L.A.'s three stars combined to create a goal. Beckham flicked the ball to Keane, who made a perfect pass to Donovan, who one-timed it into the net. The goal stood up and the Galaxy won their third MLS championship. Beckham perhaps enjoyed it the most. He had been brought to L.A. to make the Galaxy winners, but his first two seasons were disappointing. The championship gave him a title in his third pro league, joining trophies in England and Spain.

Donovan and Beckham show off their new silver.

News from the first half of MLS 2012:

✳ *Bienvenue,* Montréal! That means "Welcome!" to the 19th and newest MLS team, the Montreal Impact. In its first season, the Impact struggled on the field, but filled the stands. Montreal joined the Vancouver Whitecaps and FC Toronto as Canadian teams in Major League Soccer.

✳ 2010 and 2011 goal-scoring champ **Chris Wondolowski** of San Jose just kept right on scoring. Midway through 2012, he was averaging nearly a goal per game, well on his way to leading the league once again.

✳ Sporting KC made the semifinals in 2011, and they kept right on trucking in 2012. At the break, they led the Eastern Conference and looked like the team to beat for the MLS title.

✳ The annual MLS All-Star Game (see roster below) turned into a major triumph for MLS players. A goal in injury time by **Eddie Johnson** of the Seattle Sounders gave the MLS team a thrilling 3–2 victory over visiting Chelsea, the defending English Premier Leauge champs.

LIVERPOOL AT FENWAY

Soccer at Fenway Park? Don't they play baseball there? England's Liverpool, which is run by the Red Sox owners, played Italy's FC Roma in a game beneath the Green Monster. The "friendly" drew 37,000 soccer fans to the ballpark.

2012 Best XI

These are the top 11 MLS players chosen by fans to take part in the 2012 All-Star Game, played against Champions League winner Chelsea.

GOALIE:
Jimmy Nielson, Sporting KC

DEFENDERS:
Steven Beitashour, San Jose
Aurelien Collin, Sporting KC
Jay DeMerit, Vancouver
Heath Pearce, New York

MIDFIELDERS:
David Beckham, Los Angeles
Dwayne De Rosario, D.C.
Landon Donovan, Los Angeles
Graham Zusi, Sporting KC

FORWARDS:
Thierry Henry, New York
Chris Wondolowski, San Jose

Stat Stuff

MAJOR LEAGUE SOCCER
CHAMPIONS

2011 Los Angeles Galaxy
2010 Colorado Rapids
2009 Real Salt Lake
2008 Columbus Crew
2007 Houston Dynamo
2006 Houston Dynamo
2005 Los Angeles Galaxy
2004 D.C. United
2003 San Jose Earthquakes
2002 Los Angeles Galaxy
2001 San Jose Earthquakes
2000 Kansas City Wizards
1999 D.C. United
1998 Chicago Fire
1997 D.C. United
1996 D.C. United

World Cup Scoring Leaders

MEN

GOALS	PLAYER, COUNTRY
15	Ronaldo, Brazil
14	Miroslav Klose, Germany
14	Gerd Müller, West Germany
13	Just Fontaine, France
12	Pelé, Brazil
11	Jürgen Klinsmann, Germany
11	Sandor Kocsis, Hungary

WOMEN

GOALS	PLAYER, COUNTRY
14	Birgit Prinz, Germany
14	Marta, Brazil
13	Abby Wambach, United States
12	Michelle Akers, United States

WOMEN'S WORLD CUP
ALL-TIME RESULTS

YEAR	CHAMPION	RUNNER-UP
2011	**Japan**	United States
2007	**Germany**	Brazil
2003	**Germany**	Sweden
1999	**United States**	China
1995	**Norway**	Germany
1991	**United States**	Norway

EUROPEAN CHAMPIONSHIP

Since 1960, the national teams of European nations take part in a long series of playoffs leading to the UEFA European Championship. It was first called the Nations Cup and switched to the current name in 1968. As Spain celebrates its back-to-back titles, here's a look at all the past winners.

2012	**Spain**	1984	**France**
2008	**Spain**	1980	**West Germany**
2004	**Greece**	1976	**Czechoslovakia**
2000	**France**	1972	**West Germany**
1996	**Germany**	1968	**Italy**
1992	**Denmark**	1964	**Spain**
1988	**Netherlands**	1960	**Soviet Union**

GOLF

HE'S BACK!

Tiger Woods was the best golfer in the world for more than a decade, but he hit a rough patch. That is, until 2012 started. Woods won three events in the first half of the year, serving notice that he has designs at reclaiming his spot atop the golf world.

Tiger Roars!

The biggest news in golf in the past year has been the return of the biggest name in golf: **Tiger Woods**. After three years without a victory, Woods won three events in 2012. With a win in the Memorial in May, he tied **Jack Nicklaus** for the No. 2 spot in career PGA victories. With a win at the AT&T National in June, he passed Nicklaus. With 74 wins, Woods now trails only **Sam Snead**, who had 82 wins from 1937–65.

Woods had struggled with injuries and some off-the-course problems. Some wondered if he would ever regain the amazing form that helped him win 14 major tournaments—so far. But after rest and lots of practice, he came back swinging in 2012. Along with three wins through July, Tiger finished third at the British Open. With that win, he moved to No. 2 in the world golf rankings.

Another big story in golf was the inability of some golfers to wrap up big titles. At The Masters in April, South African **Louis Oosthuizen** had a rare double-eagle in the final round, but it wasn't enough. He was one of several players who led during the final round, but in the end it was American **Bubba Watson** who emerged from the pack. At the U.S. Open, **Jim Furyk** was in control before fading at the end. That let **Webb Simpson** swoop in for his first major victory. The British Open in July was the site of the biggest late collapse. Australia's **Adam Scott** led by four strokes with just four holes to play. Then he blew up, dropping all four strokes. He had an eight-foot putt on the 18th hole that would have given him a tie and a spot in a playoff, but he missed. Veteran **Ernie Els** won his first major in 10 years as a result.

2012 MEN'S MAJORS

THE MASTERS
Bubba Watson

THE U.S. OPEN
Webb Simpson

THE BRITISH OPEN
Ernie Els

THE PGA CHAMPIONSHIP

Chip Shots

OUCH▶▶▶

Kyle Stanley had a tournament to forget at the 2012 Farmers Insurance Open. He was ahead by as many as seven strokes in the final round. He stood on the 18th tee still leading by three. A few moments later, after hitting a shot into a lake and then three-putting, he faced a playoff. Facing **Brent Snedeker**, he missed a four-foot putt to give the win to his opponent.

◀◀◀AWESOME OPEN

Beau Hossler had a different sort of summer than most 17-year-olds. While his schoolmates were traveling or working or getting ready for senior year, Hossler was playing in the world's toughest golf tournament . . . and playing really well! He was one of two teenagers to play in the U.S. Open and for a little while on Saturday, he looked like he had a shot at winning it! A final-round 76 humbled him, but he'll always remember his first Open.

WHO'S NO. 1▶▶▶

Irishman **Rory McIlroy** and Englishman **Luke Donald** (right) played ping-pong with the World Golf Rankings. The two traded the No. 1 spot over and over through the first half of 2012. Donald pulled ahead with solid summer finishes, and then **Tiger Woods** jumped over McIlroy after the British Open. That trio should be battling through 2013 to see who is really number one.

U.S. Captures President's Cup

Led by a perfect 5–0 record from **Jim Furyk** (left), the U.S. team won the President's Cup in late 2011. The event, held every two years, pits an American team against a squad of international all-stars. Furyk won every match he played, but it was **Tiger Woods** who nailed down the trophy-clinching points. The event was held in Australia at the only course where the U.S. has lost the President's Cup, back in 1998. But five Aussie golfers could manage only five wins, and the U.S. carried the Cup on the long flight back home.

A WORLD CUP IN GOLF?

It's not just soccer that has a World Cup. Every two years, golf holds one as well. In late 2011, a pair of U.S. golfers won the event, the first American win in 11 years. **Matt Kuchar** and **Gary Woodland** held the lead over Germany and England going into the final match. A 67 in that round helped them hold on to the lead and carry home the huge World Cup trophy. England overtook Germany to finish second.

Women's Golf

W hile men's golf saw the resurgence of an old star and the emergence of some new young ones, women's golf saw a different kind of change. The LPGA held only 23 tournaments in 2011, its fewest tournaments ever. In addition, only 13 of those events were held in the United States. Also, foreign golfers have had a huge impact on women's golf in recent years. While golfers from 10 different countries won tournaments in 2011, Americans won only four. However, five U.S. golfers did finish the year among the top 10 in earnings, and in 2012 the number of U.S.-based tournaments rose to 15.

The biggest star in 2011 was **Yani Tseng** of Taiwan (right), who won two majors and five other tournaments. She finished in the top 10 in 14 of 22 tournaments! Tseng kicked off 2012 by winning three of the first five LPGA events. American **Cristie Kerr** was second on the money list, but she did not earn a victory in 2011. Fellow U.S. golfer **Brittany Lincicome**, however, won two events.

2012 Women's Majors

U.S. Women's Open: **Na Yeon Choi**

Kraft Nabisco: **Sun Young Yoo**

◀◀◀LPGA Championship: **Shanshan Feng**

British Women's Open: _____

2011 LPGA Money List

1. **Yani Tseng**, Taiwan		$2.92 million
2. **Cristie Kerr**, U.S.		$1.47 million
3. **Na Yeon Choi**, South Korea		$1.36 million
4. **Stacey Lewis**, U.S.		$1.36 million
5. **Suzann Pettersen**, Norway		$1.32 million

GOLF NOTES

SO CLOSE!
I. K. Kim just had to make one very short putt to win her first major championship, the 2012 Kraft Nabisco event. It was a putt she has probably made 10,000 times in tournaments and in practice. In golf, they call it a tap-in. But for Kim, it was a tap-out. She missed that mini-putt and had to go into a playoff. Crushed by her big miss, she lost to Sun Young Yoo.

NEW WINNER
At the Wegmans LPGA Championship in New York, the growing international crowd of golfers found a new hero. With a final-round 67, **Shanshan Feng** became the first golfer from China to win an LPGA major tournament. Feng was a star on the Japan Pro Tour, but this was her first big LPGA victory.

GREAT START!
In September 2011, **Lexi Thompson**'s (pictured) friends were all starting school. Thompson, meanwhile, was setting a record. At the LPGA's Navistar Classic in Alabama, she became the youngest winner of an LPGA event. She was just 16! A couple of months later, Thompson won the Dubai Ladies Masters to earn the same honor on the European Tour. But Lexi's record only lasted until August 2012, when **Lydia Ko**, 15, topped her. See page 183 for details.

SOLHEIM CUP
The Solheim Cup matches a team of American female golfers against a team from Europe. The U.S. had won the last three Cups, but in 2012 Europe told a different story. With a run of big wins in single matches on the last day, Europe snatched victory from defeat. Spanish golfer **Azahara Muñoz** got the last half-point to guarantee the win. American star **Michelle Wie** lost a key match to **Suzann Pettersen** of Norway after Pettersen rolled in three birdies to end their match.

The Majors

In golf, some tournaments are known as the majors. They're the four most important events of the year on either the men's or the women's pro tours. **Tiger Woods** has the most career wins in majors among current golfers. **Annika Sorenstam** retired in 2010 with the most among recent LPGA players.

MEN'S

	MASTERS	U.S. OPEN	BRITISH OPEN	PGA CHAMP.	TOTAL
Jack **NICKLAUS**	6	4	3	5	18
Tiger **WOODS**	4	3	3	4	14
Walter **HAGEN**	0	2	4	5	11
Ben **HOGAN**	2	4	1	2	9
Gary **PLAYER**	3	1	3	2	9
Tom **WATSON**	2	1	5	0	8
Arnold **PALMER**	4	1	2	0	7
Gene **SARAZEN**	1	2	1	3	7
Sam **SNEAD**	3	0	1	3	7
Harry **VARDON**	0	1	6	0	7

WORLD CUP

The past ten winners of the World Cup of Golf

2011 **UNITED STATES**	2007 **SCOTLAND**	2003 **SOUTH AFRICA**
2009 **ITALY**	2006 **GERMANY**	2002 **JAPAN**
2008 **SWEDEN**	2005 **WALES**	2001 **SOUTH AFRICA**
	2004 **ENGLAND**	

WOMEN'S

	LPGA	USO	BO	NAB	MAUR	TH	WES	TOTAL
Patty **BERG**	0	1	x	x	x	7	7	15
Mickey **WRIGHT**	4	4	x	x	x	2	3	13
Louise **SUGGS**	1	2	x	x	x	4	4	11
Annika **SORENSTAM**	3	3	1	3	x	x	x	10
Babe **ZAHARIAS**	x	3	x	x	x	3	4	10
Betsy **RAWLS**	2	4	x	x	x	x	2	8
Juli **INKSTER**	2	2	x	2	1	x	x	7
Karrie **WEBB**	1	2	1	2	1	x	x	7

KEY: LPGA = LPGA Championship, USO = U.S. Open, BO = British Open, NAB = Nabisco Championship, MAUR = du Maurier (1979–2000), TH = Titleholders (1937–1972), WES = Western Open (1937–1967)

PGA TOUR CAREER EARNINGS*

1.	Tiger Woods	$99,502,664
2.	Vijay Singh	$66,519,055
3.	Phil Mickelson	$66,298,248
4.	Jim Furyk	$51,107,109
5.	Ernie Els	$44,368,840
6.	Davis Love III	$41,868,857
7.	David Toms	$38,279,278
8.	Steve Stricker	$33,814,961
9.	Kenny Perry	$31,797,536
10.	Justin Leonard	$31,635,046

LPGA TOUR CAREER EARNINGS*

1.	Annika Sörenstam	$22,573,192
2.	Karrie Webb	$16,812,795
3.	Lorena Ochoa	$14,863,331
4.	Cristie Kerr	$13,857,805
5.	Juli Inkster	$13,394,130

* Through July 2012

LOUISE SUGGS

Women's pro golf was born in 1950 when a group of top players formed the LPGA. Louise Suggs was one of those founding members— and was one of the best players, too. Suggs won 58 pro tournaments, including 11 majors. She won the 1957 LPGA Championship, and she became the first golfer to win all four of the women's majors in her career. She was also one of the first members of the LPGA Tour Hall of Fame. Before turning pro, the Georgia native won a stack of amateur championships in the U.S. and Great Britain. Today, the LPGA Rookie of the Year receives the Louise Suggs trophy.

TENNIS

VIVA RAFAEL!
In the middle of the greatest three-man tennis battle ever, Rafael Nadal continued to dominate in Paris, winning his seventh French Open.

Three-Man Race

The merry-go-round at the top of men's tennis continued to whirl in 2012. The ride usually only has three horses, but at Wimbledon, another tried to jump into the game. Spanish star **Rafael Nadal** was ahead for a year or so, but then **Novak Djokovic** of Serbia crashed the party and won three straight Grand Slam titles. Their battles followed a longer period of success by Swiss superstar **Roger Federer**, who many experts called the greatest player ever . . . until the other two guys started beating him. The trio has been so good that in the 31 Grand Slam events leading up to the 2012 U.S. Open, Federer, Nadal, or Djokovic had won all except a single Grand Slam.

Federer won Wimbledon . . . again!

The sport continues to focus on those Grand Slam tournaments and in 2012, fans enjoyed classic matches in all of them, with one of the "big three" winning each event.

AUSTRALIAN OPEN: In what *Sports Illustrated* called an "epic final," Djokovic defeated archrival Nadal. The two played until well past one o'clock in the morning in the longest Grand Slam final ever played—it lasted nearly six hours! The action was back and forth, intense, and powerful. Some experts called it one of the greatest matches ever.

FRENCH OPEN: Two months later, however, Nadal got his revenge on Djokovic on the red clay of Paris. After Djokovic beat Federer in the semis, Nadal happily took him on. Continuing his career-long dominance on clay, Nadal won even after a rain delay sent the players home overnight. Nadal's seventh Open win in Paris set a new all-time record, too.

WIMBLEDON: Djokovic and Nadal had theirs in 2012. Would Federer get his? He went into Wimbledon with a record 16 Slams, but he had not won a Grand Slam since 2010. The other great part of the final—**Andy Murray**, Federer's opponent. No player from Great Britain has won that country's championship since **Fred Perry** in 1936. But though he had the home crowd on his side, Murray could not overcome the Swiss giant and Federer made it No. 17 and his record-tying seventh Wimbledon win.

2012 MEN'S GRAND SLAMS

AUSTRALIAN OPEN	**Novak Djokovic**
FRENCH OPEN	**Rafael Nadal**
WIMBLEDON	**Roger Federer**
U.S. OPEN	**Andy Murray**

Women's Tennis

If men's tennis was a battle between three giants, women's tennis included a mix of emerging stars and veterans returning to top form. At the Australian Open, **Victoria Azarenka** captured her first Grand Slam championship. With the win, she became the first player from Belarus to be ranked No. 1 in the world. In fact, she jumped there from No. 3 and so

was the first player to skip right over No. 2! Azarenka defeated former No. 1 **Maria Sharapova** in Melbourne, but Sharapova would have her moment in the sun soon.

It came in Paris, where the Russian star became the tenth woman to win all four of the Grand Slams in her career. Her win also capped a big comeback. She had won a trio of Grand Slams before she was 21, but a shoulder injury had knocked her out of the game and she was struggling to return to form. The French Open win also moved her back to No. 1.

At Wimbledon, the tennis world welcomed another star back to the top. **Serena Williams** beat Poland's **Agnieszka Radwanska** for her fifth title in England. That equaled the mark of her sister Venus, and was Serena's first since 2010. Williams had spent almost a year dealing with a foot injury and lung problems. She worked hard for months to return to the top of the tennis world. (She also teamed with **Venus** to win the women's doubles championship, giving the sisters 13 career Grand Slam tournament doubles titles.) She won her fourth U.S. Open, too.

Serena jumped for joy in England!

2012 WOMEN'S GRAND SLAMS

AUSTRALIAN OPEN	**Victoria Azarenka**
FRENCH OPEN	**Maria Sharapova**
WIMBLEDON	**Serena Williams**
U.S. OPEN	**Serena Williams**

TENNIS NOTES

Nadal Was Blue ▶▶▶

At the Madrid Open, organizers tried something new: blue clay on the court. It shocked tennis fans and made **Rafael Nadal** angry, especially after he lost in the final. It was so controversial that the ATP Tour said "no more blue" in 2013. Player **Ivo Karlovic** said, "It looks like something Smurfs would play on."

They Were LOUD!

If you've watched much tennis, you know that some players are, well . . . loud. They let out grunts, whoops, or other noises with each big hit. (Azarenka is famously noisy.) Some competitors and fans don't like the sounds. In June, the WTA announced that it was developing a device that would measure grunting. They're not calling it a "grunt-o-meter" but everyone else is. Once the device is in place, officials will use it to find players who are too loud. No word yet on what the penalties will be . . . or if grunters will have to play with their mouths covered!

◀◀◀ Shvedova Was Golden

Baseball has the perfect game. It's when a pitcher does not allow a baserunner while winning a nine-inning contest (see page 74). What you might not know is that tennis has the "golden set." It's very rare, but it was accomplished at Wimbledon by **Yaraslova Shvedova** on June 30. Against **Sara Errani**, she won every single point in a set—all six games and each of the four points in each game.

Stat Stuff

ALL-TIME GRAND SLAM CHAMPIONSHIPS (MEN)

	AUS. OPEN	FRENCH OPEN	WIMBLEDON	U.S. OPEN	TOTAL
Roger **FEDERER**	4	1	7	5	**17**
Pete **SAMPRAS**	2	0	7	5	**14**
Roy **EMERSON**	6	2	2	2	**12**
Björn **BORG**	0	6	5	0	**11**
Rod **LAVER**	3	2	4	2	**11**
Rafael **NADAL**	1	7	2	1	**11**
Bill **TILDEN**	0	0	3	7	**10**
Jimmy **CONNORS**	1	0	2	5	**8**
Ivan **LENDL**	2	3	0	3	**8**
Fred **PERRY**	1	1	3	3	**8**
Ken **ROSEWALL**	4	2	0	2	**8**
Andre **AGASSI**	4	1	1	2	**8**

FRED PERRY With Andy Murray earning headlines in England for his Olympic gold medal (see page 29), here's a look back at the last British tennis star to win big at Wimbledon. Perry played in the 1930s and was the first player to win all four of the Grand Slam tournaments in his career. He was ranked No. 1 in the world from 1934–36. He was also one of the first great players to turn pro. Today, a statue of him stands at Wimbledon marking his career. A popular line of tennis clothing named for him continues to sell well, too.

ALL-TIME GRAND SLAM CHAMPIONSHIPS (WOMEN)

	AUS.	FRENCH	WIMBLEDON	U.S.	TOTAL
Margaret Smith **COURT**	11	5	3	5	24
Steffi **GRAF**	4	6	7	5	22
Helen Wills **MOODY**	0	4	8	7	19
Chris **EVERT**	2	7	3	6	18
Martina **NAVRATILOVA**	3	2	9	4	18
Serena **WILLIAMS**	5	1	5	4	15
Billie Jean **KING**	1	1	6	4	12
Maureen **CONNOLLY**	1	2	3	3	9
Monica **SELES**	4	3	0	2	9
Suzanne **LENGLEN**	0	2*	6	0	8
Molla Bjurstedt **MALLORY**	0	0	0	8	8

*Also won 4 French titles before 1925; in those years, the tournament was open only to French nationals.

CAREER GRAND SLAMS

(Year represents fourth win of four Grand Slam events. Players with an * also won an Olympic gold medal.)

Maria SHARAPOVA (2012)

Serena WILLIAMS* (2003)

Steffi GRAF* (1988)

Martina NAVRATILOVA (1983)

Chris EVERT (1982)

Billie Jean KING (1972)

Margaret SMITH COURT (1963)

Shirley Fry IRVIN (1957)

Maureen CONNOLLY (1953)

Doris HART (1954)

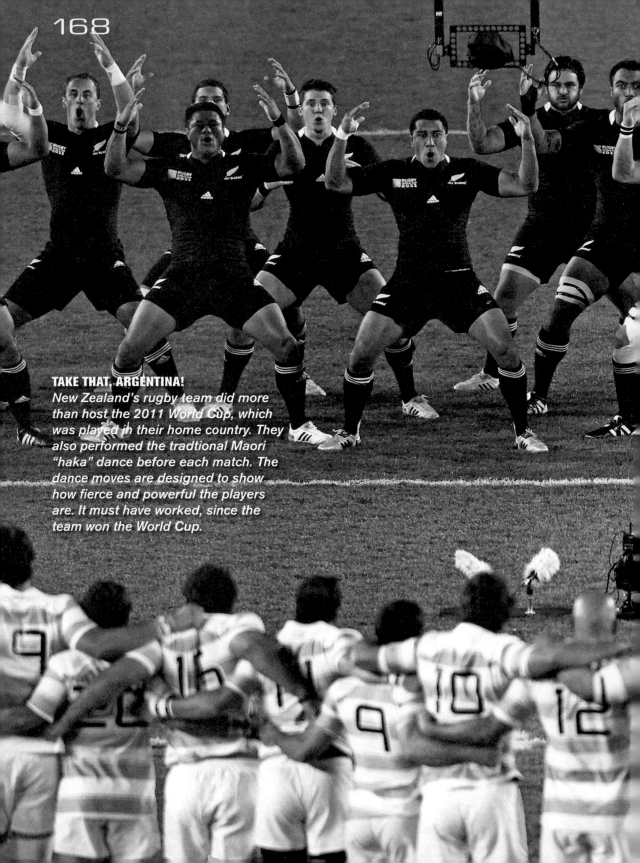

TAKE THAT, ARGENTINA!

New Zealand's rugby team did more than host the 2011 World Cup, which was played in their home country. They also performed the tradtional Maori "haka" dance before each match. The dance moves are designed to show how fierce and powerful the players are. It must have worked, since the team won the World Cup.

OTHER SPORTS

Horse Racing

I'll Have Another (purple silks) pulls away to win the Kentucky Derby.

Thousands of people flocked to New York for the Belmont Stakes. Ticket sales were huge. Millions of dollars were riding on the race. Then, a little more than 24 hours before post time came the bad news. Due to an injury to one of its feet, I'll Have Another was "scratched." That meant the horse would not run in the Belmont, nor have a chance at the Triple Crown.

The 2012 horse racing year was ALMOST amazing. A sport that was looking for a big hero to push it back to the top of the sports scene suddenly found one. **I'll Have Another** was a big winner at the Kentucky Derby, galloping to victory over **Bodemeister**.

In the Preakness Stakes, the big horse from Kentucky did it again, to many people's surprise. With a dramatic run down the stretch, I'll Have Another did just that—had another. That gave the horse and jockey **Mario Gutierrez** the first two legs of the Triple Crown. No horse has won the famous triple since Affirmed in 1978 (see box). Racing fans got super excited about the possibility of another name on that short list.

I'll Have Another was also retired from racing for good to prevent any further injury. He had a terrific run and made a lot of racing fans excited, but now he'll join everyone else in waiting for another Triple Crown winner. Maybe in 2013?

TRIPLE CROWN WINNERS
SINCE WORLD WAR II

YEAR	HORSE
1978	Affirmed
1977	Seattle Slew
1973	Secretariat
1948	Citation
1946	Assault

Six other horses won from 1919–1943.

Lacrosse

For the past few years, lacrosse has been one of the fastest-growing sports in America. The game began centuries ago as a tribal ritual among Native Americans. It is now played indoors and outdoors by young players, colleges, and the pros.

▲ NCAA

College lacrosse has boomed in popularity. More and more schools now have teams and the championships were on national TV. Loyola University Maryland ended up on top after an exciting series of playoff games. In the championship game, the Greyhounds won because of their strong defense. They held the University of Maryland team to zero goals for more than 40 minutes. The final score was 9–3. **Eric Lusby** had four of those goals to give him 17 for the championship tournament, an all-time NCAA record.

Loyola captured its first NCAA Division 1 championship in any sport. Not bad for a team that was not ranked at all before the season started!

▲ NATIONAL LACROSSE LEAGUE

Things did not look good for the Rochester Knighthawks at halftime of the National Lacrosse League's Champion's Cup final. They trailed the Edmonton Rush by four goals as the two teams battled during the indoor game.

Things looked a lot better less than a half hour later. The 'Hawks scored seven goals to open the second half while allowing none in that stretch. They never looked back and won their third NLL championship.

Cody Jamieson of Rochester had four goals and four assists, and was named the Champion's Cup MVP as Rochester won, 9–6.

BAYHAWKS ARE BEST!

Ben Hunt had four goals, and they played a big part in giving the Chesapeake Bayhawks their fourth Major League Lacrosse (MLL) title. The Bayhawks defeated the Denver Outlaws 16–6 in a game played at Harvard Stadium, near Boston. Chesapeake also won championships in the outdoor lacrosse league in 2002, 2005, and 2010.

Boxing

Manny Pacquiao of the Philippines is considered probably the best overall boxer in the world. Though fighting at only about 140 pounds, he's a powerful fighter who is a national hero in his home country. He even ran for the national legislature and won a seat there. He has earned titles in eight different divisions, the most of any fighter ever. The Boxing Writers Association named him the fighter of the decade for the 2000s.

Bradley was a surprise winner.

When he faced **Timothy Bradley** of the United States in one of the biggest boxing matches of 2012, most people expected Pacquiao to add to his amazing record. When the fight was over, however, the judges disagreed. In a very controversial decision, they chose Bradley as the winner. Most experts felt Pacquiao had won, but the decision stood.

MMA

Mixed martial arts has gotten a lot more attention in recent years. Several groups organize the fights and earn big TV ratings. The Ultimate Fighting Championships have been the busiest.

Rivalries are always a big deal in any of the fighting sports. UFC has one of the best: heavyweights **Junior dos Santos** (the fighter on the right) and **Cain Velasquez**. At UFC 146 (all the big UFC events are numbered), dos Santos knocked out Velasquez in only 64 seconds. Dos Santos most often uses boxing moves, while other fighters try to use more kicking and wrestling. He became the top-ranked heavyweight after the big win.

However, a rematch in September promised to keep the rivalry alive. If Velasquez won that battle, look for yet another matchup to decide the champ!

Rugby

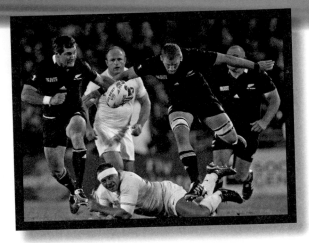

The hometown guys made good at the 2011 Rugby World Cup. The event, held every four years like its soccer counterpart, was the largest sports event ever held in New Zealand. The Kiwi fans enjoyed every minute, as their team won its second World Cup, edging France 8–7 in a dramatic final.

New Zealand had had little trouble before the final. They won all four of their pool matches, including an 83–7 whomping of Japan and a 79–15 pasting of Canada. In the quarterfinals, they had little trouble with Argentina, and then they beat archrival Australia in the semifinals, 20–6.

The championship game matched two teams with great defenses. In the end it came down to which team made the most kicks. New Zealand made theirs and France missed a couple. From the pregame "haka" dance to the final hoisting of the trophy, this World Cup was really "made in New Zealand."

Gymnastics

Jordyn Wieber proudly displayed her gold medal.

Heading into an Olympic year, the U.S. gymnastics teams, especially the women, wanted to put on a good show at the 2011 World Championships. They did that and more, winning seven overall medals including the team gold. The medal total was tied for the most ever by an American team.

Even losing team captain **Alicia Sacramone** to an injury didn't stop the women from capturing the team title. In the all-around, **Jordyn Wieber** set herself up as an Olympic favorite by narrowly winning the overall. **McKayla Maroney** also earned a gold by winning the vault event.

On the men's side, a team bronze for third was the highest finish for a U.S. men's team in a decade. **Danell Leyva** had the best individual finish, winning gold in the parallel bars.

Cycling

Tour de France

E ngland and France have a quite a relationship. For centuries they were at war with each other. For the past 300 years or so, however, they've mostly been friends. However, France still has the world's most famous cycling race, and though riders from Great Britain have taken part for decades, none of them won . . . until 2012.

With a powerful move in the mountain stages and steady success in time trials, **Bradley Wiggins** became the first person from Britain to win the fabled Tour de France.

Wiggins was dominant in time trials, the shorter days of the Tour run strictly against the clock instead of other riders. He won two of them, trailing only fellow Briton **Mark Cavendish**.

But while the two battled in the sprints, it was Wiggins's steady success in long-distance flat races and brutal moutain climbs that kept him in the lead. He took over the yellow jersey worn by the race leader on July 7 and never gave it up. After 2,100 miles, Wiggins wrote a new page in the long England vs. France story.

Wiggins led the way as the Tour de France ended in Paris.

A Future Hero

Is **Tejay van Garderen** (left) the next American Tour de France hero? In 2012, van Garderen, who is from Montana, won the white jersey given to the Tour's best young rider. He finished fifth overall, making him the favorite to take over as America's best hope in long-distance cycling.

Bowling

People have been bowling for centuries, but nearly all of them use one hand to throw the ball down the lane. That changed when Australian **Jason Belmonte** used a unique two-handed grip. He won numerous tournaments and set scoring records.

When Finland's **Osku Palermaa** won the 2012 Professional Bowlers Association World Championship, he set two big new "firsts." He was the first two-handed bowler to capture the title. He was also the first bowler from outside the United States to end up on top.

Bowling has grown internationally in recent years. Other international players have reached the PBA Tour, but Palermaa is the first to win it all. Belmonte was one of the semifinalists, too; we'll probably see more two-handers in the future.

Two hands on the ball! That's Palermaa's winning style.

Fishing

Chris Lane was worried after the eight-pound fish he thought he had hooked at the 2012 Bassmasters Classic got away. After the loss, Lane buckled down and kept casting. Two days later, he had hooked enough big and little ones to become the champion.

Lane had won four other tournaments, but this was his first in what some fans call the Super Bowl of fishing. He held off a challenging field of anglers all trying to match wits with the fish and each other. At the weigh-in, Lane's total weight of fish caught tipped the scales at 51.6 pounds. For being the best fisherman on the Red River near Shreveport, Louisiana, Lane took home $500,000.

Earlier, at the 2011 season-ending Bassmasters All-Star Championship, **Ott DeFoe** reeled in 33.4 pounds of fish on the Alabama River near Montgomery.

Lane holds up part of his Classic-winning catch.

Winter Sports

Lindsey Vonn continues her reign as the world's best female skier.

SKIING

Lindsey Vonn dominated women's skiing from 2008 through most of 2011, winning three World Cup championships. But a snowstorm wiped out the final race of 2011 and she was nipped for her fourth title by another skier. Vonn got her revenge in 2012 by becoming only the second woman to win four overall World Cup titles. She finished almost 500 points ahead of the runner-up.

Vonn succeeds by being very skilled in all of the major types of skiing—downhill, giant slalom, and slalom. Many skiers excel in one or two, but Vonn is one of the best in all three. This versatility has made her the top American woman skier of all time.

In 2012, she was the overall champion in downhill, combined, and Super G, and finished second in giant slalom. **Julia Mancuso** finished fourth overall as the next highest American.

Meanwhile, another American skier was setting a record of her own. By winning the moguls in China, **Hannah Kearney** set a new mark with 15 straight World Cup event wins. That broke a record set by the great **Ingemar Stenmark**, a downhill racer. Kearney won the 2012 world title in her sport, too.

On the men's side, Austrian **Marcel Hirscher** won the overall title. He beat **Beat Feuz** of Switzerland by only 25 points. That's more evidence of just how dominating Vonn was on the women's side. The top American male was slalom specialist **Ted Ligety**, who finished ninth overall.

OVERALL WORLD CUP TITLES

6	**Annemarie MOSER-PROELL**, Austria
5	**Marc GIRARDELLI**, Luxembourg
4	**Lindsey VONN**, USA
	Gustav THÖNI, Italy
	Pirmin ZURBRIGGEN, Switzerland
	Hermann MAIER, Austria

Viva Carolina! Viva Italia!

❝❝I trained so hard and I have beautiful programs. My main goal was to show how much I love figure skating.❞❞ — CAROLINA KOSTNER

FIGURE SKATING

Two years after and two years before a Winter Olympics, the 2012 World Figure Skating Championships give fans a look at who might have their eye on gold in 2014. At the event in France, Canadian skater **Patrick Chan** took home the top prize for the second year in a row. **Jeremy Abbott** was the top American, finishing eighth.

The women's winner was a bit of a surprise. **Carolina Kostner** had been taking part in international events for more than a decade without a major victory. But at this event, she won the free skate and earned enough points for her first World Championship. It was also the first world title for a female skater from Italy, and the first for a European woman since 2005. **Ashley Wagner** of the United States just missed out on a medal, finishing fourth.

In the pairs event, **Aliona Savchenko/ Robin Szolkowy** from Germany did it again, winning their fourth World title.

American ice dancers **Meryl Davis** and **Charlie White** could not repeat their 2011 World Championship. They finished second to Canada's **Tessa Virtue** and **Scott Moir**.

IDITAROD

Dallas Seavey knows his way around Alaska. He moved there when he was five years old and watched his dad race in numerous Iditarods. The superlong dogsled race tests man and dog alike. Dallas's dad won in 2004. In 2005, Dallas, 18, became the youngest musher to finish the race.

In 2012, Dallas matched his dad, winning his first Iditarod and becoming, at 25, the youngest ever to win. He and his team of dogs took just over nine days to complete the 975-mile race. He's not just good at mushing, either. Dallas was a high school state champion wrestler.

AMAZING SPORTS

WATER SKI RECORD

Some sports just don't fit in our other categories. This section fills you in on some amazing sports feats, plus takes a look at some young athletes making their marks. First, though, we've seen water-skiing pyramids, we've seen water-skiing Santas and we've even seen a water-skiing squirrel. Yawn. How about 145 water skiers pulled by one boat? On January 31, 2012, in Australia, the previous world record of 114 was shattered by what started out as 154 skiers (nine fell; they were not hurt).

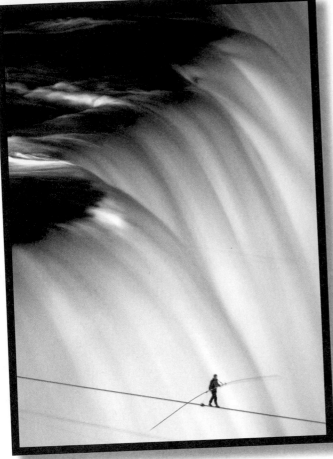

◀◀◀He Stayed Up ...

Millions of tons of water pour over Niagara Falls every day, but before June 15, 2012, no one had ever walked over it. **Nik Wallenda**, part of a long line of tightrope walkers in his family, successfully made the dangerous walk high above the crashing falls. He made the longest and widest crossing of the falls ever, taking 34 minutes to gingerly make his way across. Millions of people watched on live TV as he put one foot in front of another over and over again. He carried a long balancing pole, though the TV folks did make him wear a safety. Even with that, it was an amazing feat.

❝❝I feel like I'm on cloud nine right now. The impossible is not quite the impossible if you set your mind to it.❞❞ – NIK WALLENDA

...He Fell Down ▶▶▶

Stunt men make high falls all the time. They plunge from heights onto special air bags or huge stacks of boxes. But stuntman **Gary Connery** topped all those brave men and women. On May 23, 2012, he leaped from a helicopter hovering 2,400 feet above the ground . . . without a parachute! Connery was using a special wing suit. By extending his arms and legs, he could soar like a flying squirrel. He was still falling, though! But he used his skill and bravery to slow himself enough that when he smacked into a huge pile of boxes, all he broke was his fall.

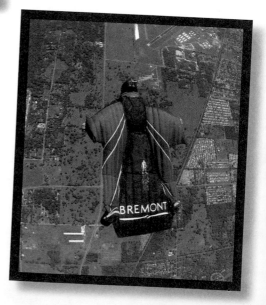

A Record to Shoot For

Combining physics, practice, and the arm of a pro quarterback, a new record for the longest paper airplane flight was set in 2012. **Joe Ayoob** was the arm—he played at Berkeley and later in a pro minor league. **John Collins** was the airplane designer. On February 29, 2012, Ayoob, after some practice flights, flung Collins's plane in an aircraft hanger in Sacramento, California. Then, 226 feet, 10 inches later, they had earned a Guinness World Record.

THANKS, MOM!

Running a marathon is one of sports' toughest tests. Giving birth is one of life's. At the 2012 Chicago Marathon, **Amber Miller** almost combined the two. The 27-year-old runner completed the 26-mile run in six hours, 23 minutes. That night, she gave birth to a baby girl! "It was the longest day of my life," Miller told the *Chicago Tribune*.

Kicking Long!

Their legs were sore, their hands ached, but the ball was still bouncing at the end! In Connecticut in 2012, two teams set a Guinness World Record for the longest kickball game of all time. While raising more than $40,000 for cancer research, the two teams played for 54 hours! They squeezed in 345 innings kicking, running, catching, and eating when they could get a break.

Kid Sports Stars

A big batch of kids accomplished amazing feats recently. Here's a look at a few young stars of today . . . and tomorrow.

3 Times Around ▶▶▶

In skateboarding, making a complete spin is a 360. Doing it twice is a 720. Doing it three times is just about impossible. Hundreds of genius boarders have tried this move, but none could do it. That is, no one could until 12-year-old **Tom Schaar** became the first ever to land a 1080. He thrilled the skateboarding world by sticking it in Tehachapi, California, on March 30, 2012. Already a gold medalist in vert competitions, Tom was among the finalists at the 2012 Summer X Games Big Air contest, an amazing result for such a young skater.

Top of the World!

In November 2011, **Jordan Romero**, 15, climbed the Vinson Massif in Antarctica. That made him seven-for-seven and the youngest person to climb the tallest mountain on each of Earth's continents. He climbed the first of the big seven, Mt. Kilimanjaro in Africa, when he was 10. He conquered Mt. Everest, the world's tallest mountain, when he was just 13!

Ski Star ▲

Aaliyah Yoong Hanifah of Malaysia is just a regular kid . . . who happens to be one of the best water skiers in the world. She was only eight years old in 2012 when she became the youngest water ski champion ever at the Southeast Asian Games. Aaliyah won the water ski tricks event.

Fore! Teen!

At only 14 years old, **Andy Zhang** became the youngest golfer in the history of the famous U.S. Open. Andy shot 79–77 in the first two rounds, so he didn't make the cut. But he loved his Open experience so much, he hopes to return another year. And though meeting and playing against the world's best

Now That Took Guts

The Santa Ana Valley High School girls' water polo team won their second straight division title in March 2012. So why do they get a mention here? Because when all the students started high school, none knew how to swim. Said one college coach, "That's epic. That's unbelievable." But it was true. Santa Ana coach Fred Lammers welcomed any student to try out. Seven brave girls gave it a shot, worked hard to learn to swim, and became water polo stars.

golfers was a thrill, he was happy about other things. "The free food is really good, too. And great candy bars in the locker room," Zhang said. "Your shoes are free and they do your laundry and everything." Nice deal!

In women's golf, another teenager made an even bigger splash. In August at the Canadian Women's Open on the LPGA Tour, **Lydia Ko** won by three strokes. No big deal, right? It was a big deal—Lydia is only 15. She became the youngest person ever to win a pro golf event.

Cool Climber ▶▶▶

One of the best bouldering and climbing athletes in America is just starting junior high. **Ashima Shirashi** is the 2012 youth national champion, but she's good enough to challenge adult climbers. In 2011, she climbed a rockface called the Crown of Aragorn in Texas. It's rated as a V13 climb; the first female *ever* to complete a V13 climb did it just two years ago and was 27. Ashima has already checked that off her list. Climbing fans can't wait to see what she'll tackle next.

Sports Internet List!

MAJOR SPORTS WEBSITES

These are the "Big Five" of professional sports leagues. Each of these websites includes links to the individual websites of the teams in the league, plus bios of top players, video clips, schedules of games, even how to find tickets!

Major League Baseball
www.mlb.com

National Football League
www.nfl.com

National Basketball Association
www.nba.com
www.wnba.com

Major League Soccer
www.mlssoccer.com

National Hockey League
www.nhl.com

OTHER SPORTS LEAGUES

Check out these websites for schedules, results, and info on athletes in your favorite sports featuring individual competitors.

Action Sports
www.allisports.com

Bowling
www.pba.com

Drag Racing
www.nhra.com

Golf
www.pgatour.com
www.lpga.com

Editor's Note for Parents and Teachers: These websites are for information purposes only and are not an endorsement of any program or organization over others. We've made every effort to include only websites that are appropriate for young sports fans, but the Internet is an ever-changing environment. There's no substitute for parental supervision, and we encourage everyone to surf smart . . . and safe!

Ice Skating
www.usfigure
skating.org

IndyCar Racing
www.indycar.com

**Motocross/
Supercross**
www.supercross.com

Stock Car Racing
www.nascar.com

Surfing
www.aspworldtour.com

Tennis
www.atpworldtour.com
www.wtatennis.com

COLLEGE SPORTS

Follow your favorite team's road to the football BCS championship or the basketball Final Four with these major college sports sites. You can find links to the schools that are members of these conferences.

Bowl Championship Series
www.bcsfootball.org

Atlantic Coast Conference
www.theacc.com

Big East Conference
www.bigeast.org

Big Ten Conference
www.bigten.org

Big 12 Conference
www.big12sports.com

Conference USA
www.conferenceusa
.com

Mid-American Conference
www.mac-sports.com

Mountain West Conference
www.themwc.com

Pac-12 Conference
www.pac-12.org

Southeastern Conference
www.secdigitalnetwork
.com

Sun Belt Conference
www.sunbeltsports.org

Western Athletic Conference
www.wacsports.com

National Collegiate Athletic Association
www.ncaa.com
This site features information about all the college sports championships at every level and division.

MAJOR SPORTS EVENTS

You'll find links to most big-time events—like the Super Bowl, the World Series, or the NBA Finals—on those sports' league websites. But here are several more world-wide sporting events that are worth a bookmark.

Little League World Series
www.littleleague.org/worldseries/index.html

The Masters
www.masters.com

Tour de France
www.letour.fr/us

Winter Olympics (2014)
www.sochi2014.com

Summer Olympics (2016)
www.rio2016.org.br/en

World Cup Soccer (2014)
www.fifa.com/world-cup/index.html

Women's World Cup Soccer (2015)
www.fifa.com/womensworldcup/index.html

World Baseball Classic
www.worldbaseball-classic.com

X Games
www.espn.go.com/action/xgames

YOUTH SPORTS ORGANIZATIONS

Rather play than watch? These websites can help get you out on the field!

Baseball
www.littleleague.org

Basketball
www.njbl.org

Football
www.usafootball.com

Golf
www.juniorlinks.com

Ice Hockey
www.usajuniorhockey.com

Soccer
www.ayso.org

Tennis
www.usta.com

MEDIA SITES

If you're looking for the latest scores or news about your favorite sport, try some of these websites run by sports cable channels or sports publications.

CBS Sports
www.cbssports.com

ESPN
www.espn.go.com

FOX Sports
www.msn.foxsports.com

Sporting News Magazine
www.aol.sportingnews
.com

Yahoo! Sports
www.sports.yahoo.com

SPORTS HISTORY

It seems like big fans know all there is to know about the history of their favorite sports. Learn more about yours at any of these websites that take you back in time.

Hickok Sports
www.hickoksports.com

Retrosheet (Baseball)
www.retrosheet.org

Sports Illustrated **Vault**
www.sportsillustrated
.cnn.com/vault

Sports Reference Family of Sites
www.baseball-
reference.com

www.basketball-
reference.com

www.pro-football-
reference.com

www.hockey-
reference.com

www.sports-reference
.com/olympics

PLAYERS ASSOCIATIONS

You're probably a little young to think about making money playing a sport. But if you're interested in the business side of things or want to discover more about what it's like to be a pro athlete, these sites may help.

MLB Players Association
www.mlbplayers
.mlb.com

NBA Players Association
www.nbpa.org

NFL Players Association
www.nflplayers.com

NHL Players Association
www.nhlpa.com

MLS Players Union
www.mlsplayers.org

GAMES

Finally, check out these sites for some rainy-day sports fun and games on the computer.

www.nflrush.com

www.sikids.com

Big Events 2012-13

September 2012

5 Football
NFL regular season begins

8–9 Tennis
U.S. Open final matches,
New York, New York

9 Cycling
Mountain Bike World
Championships, final day,
Saalfelden Leogang, Austria

20–23 Golf
Tour Championship, PGA
Atlanta, Georgia

27 Basketball
WNBA playoffs begin

27–29 Wrestling
World Championships,
Strathcona County, Canada

28–30 Golf
Ryder Cup, Medinah, Illinois

October 2012

5 Baseball
MLB postseason begins
(Wild Card playoff games,
League Division Series,
League Championship Series,
World Series)

The last time the Ryder Cup was held on U.S. soil was in 2008; the Americans won.

13 Swim/Bike/Run
Ironman Triathlon World
Championship, Hawaii

November 2012

4 Running
New York City Marathon

18 NASCAR
Ford 400, final race of Chase
for the Cup, Homestead,
Florida

30 College Football
Pac-12 Championship Game,
Site TBD

December 2012

1 College Football
ACC Championship Game,
Charlotte, North Carolina
Big Ten Championship Game,
Indianapolis, Indiana
SEC Championship Game,
Atlanta, Georgia

1 Soccer
MLS Cup, Site TBD

2 College Soccer
Women's championship game,
San Diego, California

9 College Soccer
Men's championship game,
Hoover, Alabama

January 2013

1 College Football
Rose Bowl, Pasadena, California
Orange Bowl, Miami, Florida

Stanford's women beat Duke 1–0 to win the 2011 College Cup (the NCAA soccer title).

2 College Football
Sugar Bowl, New Orleans,
Louisiana

3 College Football
Fiesta Bowl, Glendale, Arizona

5–6 NFL
Wild Card Playoff Weekend

7 College Football
Bowl Championship Series
National Championship Game,
Miami, Florida

12–13 Football
NFL Divisional Playoff Weekend

14–27 Tennis
Australian Open

20 Football
NFL Conference Championship
Games

20–27 Figure Skating
U.S. Figure Skating
Championships,
Omaha, Nebraska

Oklahoma City's Kevin Durant was the MVP of the NBA All-Star Game in 2012.

24–27 Action Sports
Winter X Games 17, Aspen, Colorado

27 Football
AFC-NFC Pro Bowl, Honolulu, Hawaii

27 Hockey
NHL All-Star Game, Columbus, Ohio

February 2013

3 Football
Super Bowl XLVII, New Orleans, Louisiana

17 NBA
NBA All-Star Game, Houston, Texas

24 NASCAR
Daytona 500, Daytona Beach, Florida

March 2013

10–17 Figure Skating
World Figure Skating Championships, London, Ontario, Canada

20–22 Action Sports
Winter X Games Europe 2013, Tignes, France

TBA* Baseball
World Baseball Classic, Championship Round, San Francisco, California

April 2013

6–8 Basketball
NCAA Men's Final Four, Atlanta, Georgia

7–9 Basketball
NCAA Women's Final Four,
New Orleans, Louisiana

11–14 Golf
The Masters, Augusta, Georgia

20 Basketball
NBA playoffs begin

TBA* Hockey
NHL playoffs begin

May 2013

4 Horse Racing
Kentucky Derby, Churchill
Downs, Louisville, Kentucky

18 Horse Racing
Preakness Stakes, Pimlico
Race Course, Baltimore,
Maryland

26 Auto Racing
Indianapolis 500, Indianapolis,
Indiana

June 2013

6–9 Golf
LPGA Championship, Henrietta
and Pittsford, New York

8 Horse Racing
Belmont Stakes, Belmont Park,
Elmont, New York

8–9 Tennis
French Open, final matches,
Paris, France

13–16 Golf
U.S. Open Championship,
Ardmore, Pennsylvania

15 College Baseball
College World Series begins,
Omaha, Nebraska

24 Tennis
All England Championships at
Wimbledon begins

27–30 Golf
U.S. Women's Open,
Southampton, New York

29 Cycling
Tour de France begins,
Porto-Vecchio, Corsica, France

July 2013

16 Baseball
MLB All-Star Game,
New York, New York

18–21 Golf
British Open Championship,
Muirfield, Gullane, Scotland

August 2013

TBA* Baseball
Little League World Series,
Williamsport, Pennsylvania

1–4 Action Sports
Summer X Games 19

8–11 Golf
PGA Championship,
Rochester, New York

Note: Dates and sites subject to change. *TBA: To be announced. Actual dates of event not available at press time.

Produced by Shoreline Publishing Group LLC

Santa Barbara, California

www.shorelinepublishing.com

President/Editorial Director: James Buckley, Jr.

Designed by Tom Carling, www.carlingdesign.com

The *Scholastic Year in Sports* text was written by

James Buckley, Jr.

plus **Craig Zeichner** and **Zachary Vanderberg** (NHL), **Jim Gigliotti** (Action Sports)

Thanks to Brenda Murray, Alix Inchausti, Marisa Polansky, Steve Diamond, Deborah Kurosz, and the all-stars at Scholastic for all their gold-medal-winning help!

Photo research was done by the authors. Thanks to Vikii Wong of Scholastic Picture Services for her assistance in obtaining the photos.

• •

Photography Credits

Front and back cover: All from **Corbis** except White and Vonn (Getty Images).

Interior:

AP/Wide World: 9, 37 bottom, 41 top, 47 bottom, 52 left, 54 bottom, 55 bottom, 58 (2), 66, 69 top, 74 top, 83 top, 85 bottom right, 89 (2), 99 (2), 115, 136, 138 (2), 139, 140, 142 (2), 144, 171 (2), 149 bottom, 156 top, 158 bottom, 173 top, 177 bottom, 180 top, 181, 188, 189

Getty Images: 4, 5, 8, 11, 14, 15, 20, 23 bottom, 25, 27, 28, 34, 35, 36 (2), 37 top, 39 bottom, 40 bottom, 41 bottom, 44 top, 45 bottom, 46 top, 47 top, 50, 52 bottom, 53, 54 top, 55 top, 56 (2), 57 (2), 59 (2), 60, 61 (2), 64, 70 bottom, 71, 74 bottom, 75, 76, 82, 83 bottom, 84, 85 (top, bottom left), 90, 92, 102, 104, 106 (2), 107, 108 top, 109, 110 (2), 111, 112 (2), 113, 116, 118 (2), 119, 120 (2), 121 (3), 122 (2), 123 (2), 126, 129 (2), 130 (2), 131 (2), 133 top, 135, 141, 143, 145, 146, 147, 148, 149 top (2), 150, 151, 154, 156 bottom (2), 157 (2), 158 top, 159, 162, 163, 164, 165 (2), 168, 170, 172 bottom, 173 bottom, 174 (2), 176, 177 top, 180 bottom, 182, 183 top, 190

US Presswire: 10, 12, 13, 16, 18, 22, 23 top, 24, 26 (2), 29, 32, 38 (3), 39 top, 40 top, 42 (2), 43, 44 bottom, 45 top, 46 bottom, 67, 68, 69 bottom, 70 top, 72 (2), 73, 77 (2), 80, 86, 87 (2), 88 (2), 94 (2), 95, 96 (2), 97, 98, 100 (2), 101, 108 bottom, 128, 132, 172 top

Additional Photography:
BassMasters: 175 bottom; Kawasaki Motors Corp., U.S.A.: 133 bottom; Mark Seaton: 178; Obe and Ashima: 183 bottom; PBA LLC: 175 top